PILGRIMAGE

A Memoir of Poland and Rome

by

JAMES A.
MICHENER

Rodale Press, Emmaus, Pennsylvania

Printed in the United States of America on acid-free paper

Cover and book design by Anita G. Patterson

If you have any questions or comments concerning this book, please write:

> Rodale Press
> Book Reader Service
> 33 East Minor Street
> Emmaus, PA 18098

Library of Congress Cataloging-in-Publication Data

Michener, James A. (James Albert), 1907–
    Pilgrimage : a memoir of Poland and Rome / by James A. Michener.
        p.   cm.
    ISBN 0–87857–910–9 hardcover
    1. Poland—Description and travel—1981–   2. Rome (Italy)—
Description—1975–   3. Michener, James A. (James Albert), 1907–
—Journeys.   I. Title.
DK4081.M53   1990
914.3804'56—dc20   90–43039
                                                                    CIP

Distributed in the book trade by St. Martin's Press

2 4 6 8 10 9 7 5 3 1   hardcover

CONTENTS

INTRODUCTION

I was touched to see that Mr. Michener entitled his story about his most recent visit to the land along the Vistula river *Pilgrimage*. We are deeply moved that our country has become the goal of pilgrimages by prominent people, headed of course by our own great compatriot John Paul II.

We are always happy to welcome Mr. Michener to our country. Someone who has written such a good, honest, and important book about Poland—and that is precisely what this outstanding, world-famous writer did in his book *Poland* and has done again in *Pilgrimage*—deserves our gratitude and lasting interest.

Yes, those "dozen trips to Poland" mentioned by the author in his memoir *Pilgrimage* have borne wonderful fruit. *Poland*, his book about our country, has sold four million copies and has been translated into 14 languages. Thanks to this book, written by a foreigner (which is a fact of significance), the world now knows more about the history and culture of Poland. It was not only the writer's talent but also the political developments between the Bug and Odra rivers that made Michener's book a best-seller. I personally welcomed this fact with true satisfaction. To this very day, I am moved by the empathy with which this prominent American, a man of the world, an observer of life in many nations, treats Polish history.

Recent years have brought great change to Polish lands. These have inspired, I believe, historic events in eastern and central Europe: a people captive, isolated, and trampled for so long is wakening to life. This book is part of that awakening. Its royalties, thanks to Mr. Michener, will go to the Young Polish Writers Fund to help the development of literature in Poland.

Once again, Mr. Michener, you are always a welcome guest in our country!

Lech Walesa

PREFACE

My education in history had been such that I came to know Europe well. My writing career had placed me in intimate touch with several Iron Curtain countries. My service with the United States government had provided me with a dozen years of high-level activity defending our system from the assaults of communism. And I cherished my association with certain artists and leaders in Europe.

So when I was invited to make a journey to two centers I especially treasured—Poland and Rome—I leaped at the opportunity to revisit scenes I knew well. I had feared, for reasons to be discussed later, that I might never again be allowed to visit Poland. I was also eager to see once more two of my friends in Rome.

It was with a lively heart that I flew out of Miami for Warsaw on what I supposed was no more than an ordinary visit. I did not realize that I was engaged in what would become a spiritual and political pilgrimage.

Poland

*W*hen the London-to-Warsaw plane came in low over the flat fields of northwestern Poland, I finally acknowledged to myself that a minor miracle was about to happen. The dramatic steps leading up to it had been sometimes accidental, but more often they were the result of both intellectual insight and personal determination.

I had first come to Poland in the late summer of 1972, when I was a minor member of the corps that accompanied President Nixon on his triumphant tour of Russia, Iran and Poland. On that occasion, I had driven far out into the countryside to visit Chopin's home, an eighteenth-century castle, and an experimental station dedicated to the improvement of Polish agriculture. It was the kind of swift exploratory foray I have always liked to take when landing in a new country.

It would be false if I said that in those fleeting moments I perceived the nature of Poland, or that I then and there decided to write a long and difficult book about the nation. But it is accurate to say that this brief taste of reality whetted an appetite long concerned with the history of Central Europe. As a young historian, I had pondered the possibility of focusing on the Balkan States, for which I had strong affinity. Later, when I delved rather deeply into Turkish history, I was constantly being lured back to a study of Turkey's neighbors: Greece, Macedonia, Albania, Serbia and Bulgaria, countries that still fascinated me. In 1956, I was deeply involved in the Hungarian uprising against the Soviet Union, and reported on that heroic affair in a book that was translated into 52 different languages.

During the long nights when I prowled the Hungarian-Austrian border, helping refugees to flee their Communist oppressors, other men well trained in the history of that part of the world assured me: "Czechoslovakia will not rise to help the Hungarians. It would never dare. But keep your eye on Poland, because those people love freedom and can behave in wild and unexpected ways." Czechoslovakia did remain docile; Poland did stage its own uprising, and all of us who were helping Hungary felt a bond of brotherhood with that distant but gallant nation.

Finally, as a self-trained geographer who had conducted many studies of European geography, I had always been aware of two fundamentals about the manner in which geography dictated the unfolding of Polish history: The lack of defensible borders eastward with Russia and westward with Germany meant that Poland was constantly under the threat of invasion from these two powers; and the preposterous arrangement known as the Polish Corridor, whereby Germany cut Poland into two parts, was obviously something that could not long prevail. I had known since 1925 that Poland lived on the edge of a historical precipice, and often repeated an evaluation I first heard from an older geographer: "Either Russia or Germany could invade Poland by merely sending a postcard saying, 'We'll be coming in on Friday,' and there would be nothing Poland could do to prevent it." And since I expected Germany to take steps to expand her corridor at any moment, I was not surprised when Hitler did just that.

My visit with President Nixon rekindled those long-nurtured interests, and in succeeding years I visited Poland about a dozen times, never remaining there an entire calendar year, never taking up permanent residence, but seeing it in all seasons of the year and seeing all corners of the nation. I saw three Polands: from 1972 to 1977, a tense, occupied nation filled with people deadened by a foreign invasion and frightened by the alien dictatorship of an atheistic communism; from 1977 to 1979, a vibrant, exuberant nation delighting in newly recovered freedoms and with a population eager to talk about everything; from 1980 to 1981, a distraught land suffering from economic stagnation, political chaos, and a very real threat of immediate invasion by Russian tanks and troops to restore Soviet domination. I experienced intimately each of these radically different periods, and was amazed by the sudden shifts.

<u>The Novel</u>　　During the middle period, television producers said: "Jim, the shows you've already done on Israel, Spain, Hawaii and the South Pacific have been such a big hit that we want to do one more. Where would you advise?" They were not prepared when I replied: "Poland."

Several witnesses can testify that when I said this, the television people gasped. "No one's interested in Poland," they said. "There are no great stories there. It's a backwater. Why not choose a real land, maybe France or Italy? Japan would be stupendous. But not Poland. No history. Nothing."

When I persisted without giving reasons, one man exploded: "What in hell would lead you to pick Poland?" I replied: "Geography. Look at the map. Poland constitutes the heartland of Europe. Always has. A crossroads where dramatic things happen if you look closely. And something must explode there, sooner or later."

"You believe that?"

"With all my heart. Make that, With all my brains, because if you have any sense of history and geography, you know that this vital chunk of land has to assume major importance. If you agree to shoot a fine series on Poland, believe me, it will turn out to be the best you've done."

Against their own better judgment, they surrendered to my ardent pleadings. And the Poland segment did prove to be the best; so good, in fact, that we shot five other shows focusing on the varied arts of Poland, and this series too would win for itself a very long and treasured life in television programs throughout the world.

As a consequence of these experiences and this growing expertise, I decided to concentrate all my energies on the writing of a long novel based on the behavior of the Polish people throughout the centuries. Once again my close advisers predicted that this would be a losing assignment on the relevant grounds that no one was interested in Poland, the names of my characters would be too difficult for the average reader to follow, and my time and effort would be wasted.

Disregarding their pessimistic warnings, I dug into Polish history, biography and custom until I felt that I understood what I was dealing with, and then wrote an impassioned collection of interlocking vignettes covering a vast period of time and a multitude of crucial events. The result was the novel *Poland,* which proceeded, to the astonishment of everyone, especially the publishers and me, to become one of my most popular works, with more than three million copies distributed in English and perhaps another million in the 12 foreign languages into which it was translated.

Here I must quickly point out that these extraordinary sales were not due to the merit of my writing but to the fact that, just as the book appeared, three cataclysmic events coincided to thrust Poland into major headlines around the world: Karol Wojtyla, the cardinal of Krakow, was elected as pope; Lech Walesa was catapulted into fame as the leader of the controlled rebellion against Communist labor policies; and General Wojciech Jaruzelski became temporary dictator. Contrary to what the television people had predicted—that no one would be interested in Poland—we found that everyone was. Rarely is an ordinary book of limited inherent interest exploded into international significance by events to which it was in no way related.

Now, as my plane neared Warsaw, I mused sardonically on the strange twist of events which had brought me on this visit. When the book was published it was harshly condemned by Polish officials, and justifiably so, because the opening and closing chapters were condemnatory of communism, and no government which ruled under that banner could be expected to approve an attack upon its basic system. I was led to believe that I would never again be welcomed in Poland, and this grieved me, for I had developed an affection for this courageous, quixotic land and its obstinate, poetic people. But I had been barred from other lands about which I had written, and had concluded that that was the penalty one paid for having stuck his nose into other people's business. I was an exile who accepted the expulsion, but not happily.

The Invitation   Then, in early 1988, with glasnost shaking the Soviet Union and its satellites, exciting rumors reached me: "The Union of Polish Writers wants to invite you to visit Poland to talk with them about literature and will extend an invitation if you give them an assurance that you'll accept." My schedule was crowded with earlier obligations, but I was so eager to see familiar haunts that I returned the signal: "I'd be honored," and through intricate channels the invitation was extended. I was profoundly pleased to think that I would again see Krakow, and the Castle in Warsaw, and the little towns along the Vistula in which I had lived and worked while doing my research.

After a series of fits and starts, with my irritating everyone by being unable to give a date when I would be free, a day in November 1988 was settled on, and to my deep satisfaction we flew out of Miami to meet with the Polish writers, for whose courage and ability I had such a high regard.

The Influence of Edward Piszek   I have not revealed the most important element in my return to Poland. Long before my first trip with Nixon in 1972, I had formed a friendship with an amazing Polish-American, the Philadelphia industrialist Edward J. Piszek, born in the United States but a fanatic Polish patriot who had assisted his ancestors' motherland in so many ways that he had made himself almost a national hero. During the first half-dozen years of our acquaintanceship, I had had no active interest in visiting Poland and certainly no interest whatever in writing about it, but I had listened to his rambling accounts of life in Poland and the adventures of Polish history, and had become aware of things Polish and his relationship to them.

Perhaps it was his tales of Polish patriotism, plus my sense of geography, that inspired me to tell the television producers: "I'll do the next segment in Poland," but I can state that he was as amazed as them at my decision.

Piszek arranged the American logistics of the visit described in this book and also arranged for the presence on our entourage of our mutual friend, the great baseball player Stan Musial, a fellow Pole. He also alerted another friend of our friends to the fact that we would be flying out of the Miami airport.

Our Departure Blanka Rosenstiel, a handsome, lively Polish woman, was the widow of the immensely wealthy American metals expert, Louis Rosenstiel, who had played a major role in bringing South African mining riches to world markets. Like Piszek, she was emotionally dedicated to Polish history and culture, and performed a multitude of good works in those fields, publishing books, conducting Chopin piano competitions for young artists, and supporting any new project that might enhance Poland's good name in America.

When she heard that I was leaving on this surprising pilgrimage to a country which had only recently rejected me, she arranged for numerous representatives of the Polish community to surprise me with a farewell party at the airport; and when I entered the waiting room to find two delightful girls in native dress awaiting with bouquets of flowers, I realized that I was once more in a Polish ambience, since flowers are an essential in that life, more treasured there than in any other nation in the world.

But there was an even deeper impact than the beautiful children and their flowers, for the numerous adult Poles in the waiting room reminded me of the profound impression my novel had made in their lives: "Before, no one in America had ever read a Polish book. No one appreciated the heroic history of our people, the grandeurs of the Polish experience. All we had were cheap Polish jokes and laughter. We were so proud when your book topped the best-seller lists. We told one another: 'They're reading about the Poland we knew,' and we were so grateful that someone not a Pole had taken the trouble to tell the true story."

So in the first moments of my pilgrimage to pay my respects to Poland, I heard the song that I would hear incessantly throughout the next week: "We are so proud that you told our story. We are so grateful that you took the trouble."

Arrival
in Warsaw

When Warsaw came in sight, someone who had read the novel reminded me: "Well, now we come to the all-revealing test," and when I asked what he meant, I received a hilarious reply: "Like you wrote: The visitor can gauge how precisely welcome he is by what's waiting for him in the airport lounge. A glass of water, you're so unimportant that you might as well go back home. A glass of tea, we won't set the dogs on you. Wine, we've heard of you but we don't believe half of what they said. But if little cakes, very sweet and crunchy, are added, we're damned glad you came to visit. And if in addition to all this, they also have a plateful of little sandwiches, it means that the prime minister himself wants to be sure you're happy with arrangements."

As we descended from the plane, we speculated among ourselves as to what would be awaiting us. I suspected that since my visit had been arranged by writers, people viewed suspiciously in Poland as elsewhere, and not by the government, the best we could hope for was water and tea, but Piszek felt sure there would also be wine, which would at least be face-saving. Lo! when we moved inside there were not only tea and wine but also large plates of the most luscious cakes and cookies you ever saw, plus a bevy of children in native dress with bouquets of flowers. The visit was going to be a grand one, but, as I accepted the flowers, some killjoy at my elbow whispered: "No sandwiches." Poland might be glad to have me back, but its joy was restrained.

Not mine. I felt a surge of excitement as I moved through the familiar passages and along streets which I had once known so well. There was the palace about which I had written; over there the great dour structure built by the Russians as a testimonial to Communist power; here the very expensive and luxurious Hotel Victoria in which I had once lived when interviewing intellectual leaders; and dead ahead the classic nineteenth-century hotel I liked so much and in which I had spent my first happy weeks in Poland, the Europejski. I had been pleased to learn before leaving the States that I would again be staying in those high-ceilinged, ornately decorated rooms. The Europejski was my kind of hotel.

Reconciliation To my considerable surprise we whisked right by it and proceeded along a quiet, well-guarded street to a residence about which I had never heard and that bore no indication that it was a hotel. Here no doorman waited, no lights blazoned the existence of a reception hall, and nothing about the interior indicated what purpose the place served. As my bags were taken to my room, I was told quietly: "This is where the government lodges its important guests. Everything is at your disposal." And everything was, for when I reached my room I found it laden with eight bottles of beverages including whisky and vodka, trays full of nuts and raisins, plates of cookies, and most important of all, a small dish of exquisite design on which rested six slim, neatly made sandwiches.

It was only then that I learned a staggering fact: Quietly, so as not to arouse comment in either Poland or the United States, the invitation which had brought me home to Poland had come not from the Writers' Union but from the government itself. Alone in my room I stared at the gifts and at the patterned carpets, and tears filled my eyes. This was the experience that writers sometimes know: to write as honestly as one can about a place, to pour into a manuscript all the love and understanding and respect and empathy one can, only to have it rejected. But then to watch, as the years pass, a subtle change take place: Readers from all parts of the world begin to stream into the country one has written about with testimonials as to how deeply the book had affected them and how it had generated an understanding which had not existed before, and how that perception, gained from a mere book, had lured them to visit the country.

Belatedly, the people governing the place written about come to the realization that whereas they still did not particularly care for the book, they now perceive that it has accomplished so much good that it constitutes a kind of national treasure, whose merit could be duplicated by nothing else. So, even though the rulers might disapprove of me, they now recognized that I had written honestly and with affection, and they respected me for it.

I had had this experience in Spain, in Afghanistan, in Hungary and to a lesser degree in both Hawaii and Israel, where my books were treated roughly by intellectual leaders of those areas who lived to see both books become major factors in developing the good reputations of the area. Only in the case of my book on South Africa has no conciliatory gesture ever been made: The book was savagely condemned on publication and banned, then quietly unbanned when the government discovered that almost everyone who came to the country was reading it and gathering from it a more solid understanding of the country. I would expect, if I live long enough, to see some kind of reasonable settlement reached in that troubled land, and to be welcomed back as one who had written wisely and well of the bad years. But I often fear that time may run out on both of us before that can happen. It is for such reevaluations that writers work.

That night the reconciliation with Poland began, for I was invited to the foreign office to meet with the Honorable Tadeusz Olechowski, Poland's foreign minister. We discussed many things, including my recent visit to Cuba and Poland's steady recovery from her economic crisis of some years earlier. And it was in this friendly, wide-ranging talk that I became aware of the real miracle of my visit. Something the minister said revealed the fact that he, and all the other officials I would meet, were well aware that for the past five years I had been a senior member of America's Board for International Broadcasting. We nine men, five Republicans and four Democrats, operated the two radio stations in Munich which broadcast constantly to the nations behind the Iron Curtain: Radio Liberty to the various nationalities in the Soviet Union; Radio Free Europe to the satellite nations, including Poland, to which we broadcasted vigorously, particularly during the years of General Jaruzelski's rule. Night after night we had tried to broadcast the facts about the Polish dictatorship and its relationship with the Soviet Union. We utilized secret freedom writings that had been spirited to us, interviews with dissidents who been able to leave the country, and a network of other sources, so that sometimes our broadcasts were much fuller than those provided by the government.

We were brilliantly opposed by a man I had never met but whom I respected as a tough psychological warrior, Jerzy Urban, who not only rebutted all we had to say but also launched his own attacks against the United States. For five years I had been engaged in this radio warfare, until I sometimes felt as if I knew more about Poland than some of those living inside; and I suppose Urban felt the same about the United States, for he was a clever rascal. His government, of course, tried to block our broadcasts by technological jamming, but we devised tricks for circumventing that.

In a certain sense I could have been classified as an enemy of Poland, and Jerzy Urban did launch that accusation against our board. But I was also a proven friend, and in that ambivalent posture I would now meet with the heads of the Polish government. It was perplexing but also exhilarating, for it represented the kind of reassessment and readjustment that captures the attention of a writer, and I was not unhappy to be in the middle of such a change, especially since all my cards were now aboveboard.

The long discussion with the foreign minister was not only a surprise but also a warm signal that the government did not propose to mask the fact that I was in Poland. It was as genial as any I had shared in past years and an intimation that there might be further surprises in store.

Later that day I would meet with another cabinet member, Aleksander Kwasniewski, whose welcome was even warmer. But that was explained by the fact that with me when we met was Stan Musial, the Hall of Fame baseball player whose amazing feats and hilarious nature made him a favorite everywhere. Stan's mission to Poland was an amusing one, as explained by Piszek: "Baseball is to be a sport in the 1992 Olympics at Barcelona, and Cuban experts are training the Russians. Musial is twice as smart as any Cuban, and he'll train the Poles to beat the Russians." Stan said he doubted that any one man could make that much difference, but he was entering the competition joyously, so our joint mission was off to a flying start.

Meeting the Press   My first full day in the country was occupied with press interviews. A troop of correspondents came to the government house to query me about my novel, its acceptance worldwide, and its probable effect on American Poles. I was asked far more questions than I could answer with any authority, but throughout the interviews ran a thread of seriousness that pleased me. People truly wanted to know how a stranger like me could have penetrated Polish consciousness with such compassion, and I explained that I had talked with hundreds of Poles not only in Poland but also throughout the world, and that from such conversations, and from readings and visits to national sites, I had acquired a feeling for Polishness, a word they liked to use and that meant substantive things to them.

At one point a man asked: "But did you ever go out into the countryside? Did you get to see Poland as it really is?" I gave a response which could stand as typical for careful writers:

"We hired a helicopter, and for nine wonderful days we flew at low altitudes to every corner of Poland, from Przemysl in the southeast to the Mazurian Lakes in the northeast, and from Szczecin in the northwest to Wroclaw in the southwest. We flew to Gdansk and to the mountains near Zakopane. We flew over the rural settlements in the south near Tarnow, where the small fields are owned by individual farmers, and over the vast flat areas of the north, where huge fields belong to cooperatives in the Russian manner, and I saw the difference in agriculture.

"We landed often to make spot inspections of things which Mr. Piszek thought might interest me. We landed at Janow Podlawski, right on the Russian border, where the world's most famous stud for breeding Arabian horses is located. And we landed at Olsztyn, where we hired a car to take us to Wolfsschanze, the impregnable underground bunker from which Adolf Hitler conducted his invasion of Russia. It was a mournful place, with slabs of concrete 14 feet thick to protect against Allied bombers, should foreign intelligence ever discover the place, which they never did.

"At the end of the nine days, I do believe I knew where Poland was and what it looked like on close inspection. I also learned that you pronounce Przemysl as *Shemish,* and Szczecin, the former Stettin, as *Scheshin.* But we also motored long distances into the countryside, and on these trips I discovered beautiful old towns like Zamosc, and especially the town in which the great Potocki family lived, Lancut, which fascinated me because it was pronounced *Winesooth.* As you know if you've read the book, I wrote a great deal about Lancut."

When I finished this recitation, rather longer than reported here, the questioner said: "I wondered how you learned so much about us. The landscape? Yes. The people? I'm not so sure."

Lech Walesa on Polish Television   The next day I encountered one of those delightful experiences that come to older Americans who travel. The American ambassador, John Davis, whom I had known in Poland years before, assembled a lunch at which I could meet some of the country's intellectual leaders. It was a lively affair, because the next night, if things went well, the famous labor union leader Lech Walesa was to be allowed to debate on public television the government's official leader of labor unions, the powerful Miodowicz. And speculation was rife that the government man would annihilate Walesa, who was, after all, no more than an unemployed shipyard worker. But some at the table were more hopeful.

"Remember," they said, "that Walesa has matured in recent years. He's gained confidence. Learned to speak. We're amazed the government would risk allowing him to utilize a podium like television." But the majority opinion was that Miodowicz would make a fool of him. Many even thought the government would, at the last moment, forbid the show.

I had met Walesa once when I was doing work at the Lenin Shipyards in Gdansk. He was an insignificant worker then, but he walked with us briefly as I inspected nine ships that were being built in his yards, and he saw that I studied carefully the names of each. One ship bore a name in Roman letters, but the other eight were in Cyrillic, so it was obvious that these latter were headed for Russia. Not Walesa but another worker told me quietly: "The Soviets pay us what you call 'ten cents on the dollar' for the ships we build them."

"Then why do you build them?"

"Because they make us."

Wherever I had gone in those days it was the same. In Tarnow, boxcars carried farm produce into Russia. In Katowice, which I knew well from many visits, flatcars carried all the steel girders produced in the great Nowa

Huta plants into Russia. In Gdansk, the fine new ships sailed to Russian home ports. Sometimes it seemed that nothing that Poland produced remained at home. But those were the bad years when everything in the nation seemed to be going to hell, so perhaps things have improved since then. But to think that Lech Walesa was going to debate in public the official head of all unions was astonishing, and I hoped the meeting would go forward.

I had been warned: "Tonight at six you're to meet with the Writers' Union, so get some rest." But when I returned to the government house I found three reporters, each working against a deadline, so instead of taking the nap I needed, I talked with them. A most interesting young woman who worked for a paper in Baltimore held a long conversation in which she asked one penetrating question after another, and I became so engrossed in the perspicacity of her questions and comments that the afternoon vanished pleasantly. At the end she said: "I'll see you tonight at the Castle, in your public guise."

"Am I going to the Castle?"

"Yes, and you must be very proud."

"About what?"

Pressing her wrist to her lips, she mumbled: "I'm afraid I've said too much," and with that she left, allowing me just enough time to talk with the other two reporters, who asked good questions but who did not betray any further secrets.

<u>At the Castle</u>   It was a bitterly cold Warsaw night marked by a heavy fall of snow with sleet and occasional flashes of hail. The streets were dangerous as we eased our way toward the center of old Warsaw, and the cobbled pavement leading to the Castle—the ancient seat of Polish monarchy—was downright treacherous; this was the wintry Poland I had known so well during my researches. I looked forward to seeing once more in the Castle the amazing set of paintings done by the Venetian artist Canaletto during a prolonged visit. But when we picked our way through the mass of cars assembled there, I learned that we were late and that everyone awaited us.

Guards saluted as we entered the Castle, and others sped us along the ancient halls in which so much Polish history had taken place. Women moved forward to take my overcoat and voices urged, "Hurry! Everyone's waiting!"

I was led into a vast ballroom used principally for visiting dignitaries; the previous speaker had been Mikhail Gorbachev, who had come to elucidate certain aspects of glasnost in which the Poles were most interested, since it might affect them deeply.

It was a golden room, ornamented in the old style and flooded with light. On tapestried chairs sat four or five hundred of Poland's intellectuals, artists and political leaders. At the table where I would sit, to do what I had not the slightest intimation, presided a wonderful elderly scholar I had known during previous visits, Bolgdan Suchodolski, who immediately rapped for attention.

"Tonight we are gathered here to honor a friend of Poland," he said, and with that he nodded to a table I had not seen when entering. There sat three dignitaries from the government, headed by Prime Minister Mieczyslaw Rakowski, who rose, marched to a microphone, and said: "The Polish government is pleased to award the highest medal in its command to a man who proved his respect and affection for our nation." He then strode to a microphone standing near me, and after a prod from Professor Suchodolski, I rose. In the flick of a moment the prime minister pinned a beribboned gold medal on my left lapel, embraced me, saluted and returned to his table.

Stunned though I was, I realized that I was supposed to speak, but no one had warned me of that obligation, so I had no notes prepared. On the spur of the moment, I did what I had done in recent years when an unsteady left knee prevented me from standing erect for long periods at a podium. I said: "You will forgive me if I sit here and do not make a speech but answer whatever questions you may wish to throw at me. I am profoundly honored by this award, which reaches me as a complete surprise. It represents the kind of acceptance a writer hopes for when he does a long book like mine. I am grateful and shall prove it by the way I accept and respond to your questions."

I think that everyone in the great hall was surprised at this proposal. But in the nervous first minutes of the exchange such mature questions burst forth—focusing on the most significant problems of our time or on the intricacies of a writer's life—that the evening became a dazzling display of intelligent questions from the floor and responses as thoughtful as I could muster without ample time for polishing my replies. It was a vigorous, honest exchange of ideas, and, after the passage of nearly an hour, it was obvious that the large audience would have been willing to query me for another hour, but Professor Suchodolski wisely halted the session with one of those statements that audiences cherish: "Drinks and refreshments in the rooms below."

One of my answers is worth giving in full. A questioner who hoped to pin me in a corner in front of the government ministers, of whom some three of four were in attendance besides the prime minister, asked me a cleverly worded question relating somehow to General Jaruzelski. I responded as I would throughout the tour:

"I was in all parts of Poland in those bad months of July, August, September and October 1981, and I saw the pitiful conditions in this land. Nothing in the stores. No food in the markets. In one restaurant after another only one dish, lunch or dinner, noodles with scraps of meat, and heavy emphasis on the noodles. Correction, we did have good breakfasts: eggs, a corner of ham, lots of fine dark toast and plenty of jam and tea. Each morning we ate like pigs for we knew that during the rest of the day we would go hungry.

"It was obvious in those last weeks that there had to be trouble in Poland, and I supposed that Soviet troops would be in Warsaw before Christmas. When General Jaruzelski assumed command a few days after I left, I was immensely relieved that it was he and not the Russians, for I better than almost any other foreigner appreciated what a perilous condition Poland had been in that autumn."

Looking in the direction of the prime minister, I continued: "In the years that followed, I never said a word about General Jaruzelski or about the semi-dictatorship that he imposed, even though I was asked repeatedly to do so, because I had seen Poland at its nadir, close up, in varied parts of the country, and I understood what the alternatives were. I thanked God that the dangers I saw were avoided.

"Many things I have seen in recent years I have not liked, but I did like the relative sanity that prevailed, the recovery of stability and the improvement of living conditions. And I am gratified that we now have an American ambassador once more in residence here. I am especially reassured because you have brought me here tonight for the bestowing of this handsome medal."

Scholarships for Polish Writers

As the evening ended, Ed Piszek, well known to many of the Poles present, rose for a short announcement: "You may wonder why Mr. Michener's books are not circulated in your country. When he worked here he helped two fine scholars translate into Polish his *Centennial* and *Space,* two of his books I'm sure you'll like. International copyright squabbles prevented their publication, but this afternoon we resolved those difficulties. The books will be printed immediately, and Mr. Michener has said that he would feel uneasy taking any money from a nation with which he feels such a close bond. He will leave all his royalties here in Warsaw, and they'll be used as scholarships for promising young Polish writers."

"What about the real novel, *Poland?*" someone asked. Piszek replied: "Same blockage up to now. In fact, when the first two couldn't be published, no one saw any reason to translate the third."

From the audience a man rose and spoke: "As a gesture of Polish-American friendship, I will pay for the translation if someone will agree to publish immediately."

Another man from the audience: "I will guarantee publication." And Piszek said, tentatively: "And I feel sure that Jim would want to assign those royalties also to the scholarship fund." I then made my closing remarks: "Do turn them over, right now, because as a boy I listened to my mother read aloud *Quo Vadis* by your Henry

Sienkiewicz, and much later I discovered your fine Nobel Prize winner, Wladyslaw Reymont, whose great novel about peasant life, *Chlopi,* influenced my attitudes toward long books and family chronicles. I owe those men an enormous debt. Perhaps one of our scholarship winners will follow them with his or her own good book."

With that we traipsed below to arched medieval caverns where rich delights were spread and goblets filled. As always on such occasions I was ravenously hungry, for I never eat before I might have to speak, but I was allowed nothing to eat by the groups that clustered about. One beautiful young woman gave me a kiss before revealing: "I played the doomed heroine in *Chlopi*"—she pronounced it accurately as *Woe-pee*—"and I am so proud that you remember Reymont."

I then told the group: "When there was a rumor in Hollywood that an epic movie was to be made of *Quo Vadis,* Sam Goldwyn said: 'They can get the money easy enough but who they gonna get to play Quo?'" The joke lost something in translation, but not my confession: "Let's not make too much about the scholarship fund. According to Polish law, I'd have to leave about 90 percent of my zloties in Poland anyway. I'm not giving up much."

What does a man do when he is back in his room alone with a medal like mine, a gorgeous thing of eagles and gold and braid? He carefully unpins it from his lapel, replaces it in its box, studies the little rosette which comes with it for wear when he doesn't wear the medal itself, and closes the cover, rarely to see the medal again. But he files in the most vital recesses of his memory the fact that a government which had rejected him at the start, with every reason to continue to do so, for he had in a sense worked against it, had the magnanimity to take him to its heart as he had taken Poland to his.

Our Team   The target had been Poland, not the acceptance of some medal, and on succeeding days our team motored to two distant cultural centers for meetings with people who wanted to talk about Poland or exhibit their arts. The first was to Lublin to the east, the second to Poznan in the west, and each was worth the trip, but for curious reasons which had not been planned.

Since we were a team in everything we did, I had better introduce the members formally. Ed Piszek was in charge, with Stan Musial as his second in command, and a more genial sports hero I cannot imagine. I had worked intimately with him in 1960 striving to elect John F. Kennedy to the presidency; we campaigned together in nine crucial states, trying to get public attention when local candidates could not, and we lost every state in which we spoke. Musial says ruefully: "If they'd sent us to two more states, Kennedy would have lost the election."

I was the third member, followed by a delightful Polish-American priest, Father Walter Ziemba of St.

Mary's College in Orchard Lake, Michigan, who conducted the various masses our Catholic members attended.

Jim Murray, former general manager of the National Football League Eagles, and originator and president of the International Advisory Board for the Ronald McDonald House, was our fifth member. Jim, a lovable leprechaun who earned the name Chiclets with his broad Irish smile, served as surrogate altar boy at masses conducted for our group.

Business affairs like passports, tickets and hotel assignments were attended to by Frank Keenan, a long-time business associate of Ed's. And keeping all things in order was Piszek's quiet son-in-law, Bob Reitenbaugh, a skilled photographer. Musial was accompanied by another baseball hero, a tall, wily fellow with a lively tongue, Larry Christenson, who helped the Phillies win a world championship. The most surprising member was Tom O'Leary, an Irish tenor with a high, sweet voice of operatic quality. He sang at the masses and at varied social affairs. He was known irreverently as our canary, which prompted me to recall one of the notable headlines in newspaper publishing. England's poet laureate—I think it must have been John Masefield—had been asked to write a laudatory poem for some insignificant event and had refused. Reported the paper: "King's Canary Won't Chirp."

The most valuable member of the team was a Warsaw Pole with whom we had all worked for many years,

Stanley Moszuk, a factotum who made the ingenuity of the Barber of Seville seem unimaginative. At various times, well-meaning friends assured me that Moszuk was an operative for the FBI, an agent of the Polish secret police, or a plant of the Russian KGB, and I believed each of them in turn. I knew him well as Moszuk, the man who could arrange anything and did.

Expedition to Lublin

We were a formidable team, and our visit to Lublin exemplified all we did. I had worked for several weeks in the city while researching my novel, and had known in terrible detail the brutal behavior of the German Nazis, for in this rural capital they showed no mercy. While our other members paid major attention to the remarkable Catholic university there, a school allowed to function vigorously even though the state frowned on religion—Pope John Paul II had been a professor there and was still carried on the roster as if absent for brief duties elsewhere—I slipped away to remind myself of the underground torture chambers in which the Nazis had killed so many local residents.

And then on a cold, blustery day, I went eastward to one of the hideous hellholes operated by the Nazis: huge, bleak Majdanek concentration camp, about which I had written in such painful detail. Since the time I had worked there, many of the hateful buildings had been torn down, but the commanding officer's house still stood, as did the crematorium. The horror of Majdanek, as I explained, was that it was so normal, so banal. There were no specific torture chambers, no German monsters running wild, nothing that one would term bizarre or the product of a diseased mind. All that happened at Majdanek was that some 450,000 were brought in—Poles as well as Jews and Gypsies—and all were murdered without great show or panoply. About half were killed immediately upon arrival, gassed primarily, with their corpses quickly carted off to ovens where they were reduced to ash. Those allowed to live were herded into long huts where they slept on the ground, often with no blankets. These died more slowly, but in the end they too went into the ovens.

At the terrible camps like Auschwitz and Treblinka, screams of the tortured still seem to hang in the air. That is not the case at Majdanek: There a low, incessant moan hangs over the sight, the sobbing of those slain in an orderly, well-managed way. To see its awful remnant when one has understood its reality is to stand silent in the face of a human aberration that has known no equal. I saluted the dead, and the vanished buildings I had known so well, and left.

There was a magical surprise in Lublin: a gala performance of local folk dancers, a team of some 40 men and women in native costume accompanied by a rural band.

The dancers performed with such tremendous vitality that even the watchers became exhausted; I had never seen anything like it. At one point, when all the bodies were whirling, the frail women suddenly grabbed the heavy men, who swung their legs out parallel to the floor while the women pirouetted with the men hanging on to them. How they did this I could not decipher, but since they did it three different times, with the small women sustaining the heavy men without falling, I can aver that they knew some trick I didn't. It was a wild, beautiful performance that erased the horror of nearby Majdanek, for it typified the vibrant continuity of life whereas the prison camp had reeked of death.

Lech Walesa Triumphant   That night we enjoyed a remarkable surprise that none of us will forget. Archbishop Bronislaw Dabrowski, custodian as it were of the hundred or more Polish bishops and a longtime holder of that elective post, hosted a formal dinner at which he spoke warmly of the contribution I had made to Poland's good reputation in the world. But I noticed that he was distracted by a young priest who ran in to give him whispered reports on some issue of magnitude. Only when the dinner ended did I learn that the famous Walesa-Miodowicz debate had been allowed to appear on national television; and when we gathered informally after the meal, there was great rejoicing, for the young priests assured us: "Walesa bested him on every point! It was a massacre, and our side won!"

Then we heard a quiet commotion outside the archbishop's residence, for in the street were many of the faithful coming to congratulate Dabrowski on Walesa's great victory, which they interpreted also as a victory for the Church. We returned inside and were in the process of saying farewell when there came a real commotion, and into the room, not ten minutes after the completion of his debate, burst Lech Walesa, flushed with victory. Hurrying directly to the archbishop, he embraced him and accepted his blessing. Then he spotted his old friend Piszek and embraced him, saying: "If I come to the United States I shall rely on you to keep me out of trouble." He could not have remembered me from Gdansk, but when he was told who I was he gripped my hands in thanks, and then he almost danced in joy at having come out of the debate unscathed.

I refer to this incident for two reasons. First, after his victory he reported first to his spiritual leader as if he, too, interpreted his good luck as a victory for the Church; and his appearance was so different from anything I had seen before that I was stunned by the transformation. He was now a world leader, a Polish charismatic, and he knew it. Dressed in a stylish suit, his hair attended to, his mustache trimmed, his posture more commanding, he was no longer a Polish peasant working at a minor job in a shipyard. He had become Lech Walesa, Nobel Prize laureate, spokesman for workers, a formidable man with whom both the Polish and Russian governments must grapple. He was the new Poland based firmly on the old.

He was with us only a few minutes, but they were electrifying, and as I watched him I thought: "He's a man soaring 15 feet in the air." I had the curious feeling that he was some notable opera star who had come into Sardi's theatrical restaurant on Broadway at the end of the grand performance to receive the applause and adulation of the crowd awaiting him there. It was a night of triumph such as few men experience, and he knew this and was relishing it.

Immediately after he left, we went to a room in the archbishop's palace to watch a videotape of the debate, which ran 45 minutes. I listened carefully as Father Ziemba at my elbow translated the arguments of Walesa and Miodowicz, the government spokesman, and I found the latter much abler than the young priests had reported when claiming that Walesa had swamped him. Miodowicz argued carefully and effectively in defense of the government-imposed union, and called effectively for loyalty to General Jaruzelski's efforts to maintain order in the workplace and in all other aspects of Polish life. He was by no means either implacable or an oaf.

But Walesa was almost majestically effective as he defended—in simple terms everyone could understand—

personal freedom, family values and the right of labor to govern its own affairs. Again and again he scored major points relating to human values, and I thought: "How similar to the Bush-Dukakis debates. Dukakis-Miodowicz had all the abstract points; Bush-Walesa controlled the emotional issues." In that sense Walesa won a notable victory, and the people of Poland knew it.

Surprises
in Poznan

Our visit to Poznan, the historic city to the west where German and Polish values often contested for superiority, was a treat. I inspected the town's ancient structures, still well preserved, served as guest of honor at a fine banquet, and met with some three dozen artists, cultural and political leaders of the area for a two-hour interrogation in which we covered questions of mutual interest. I remember this as the intellectual highlight of the entire trip, for we were dealing with subject matter of relevance to artists of all categories, and I doubt if I ever presented my basic attitudes toward art with more clarity or simplicity. We were brothers in art, those men and women of Poznan, and I thanked them for the seriousness with which they approached artistic problems, for this encouraged me to do the same. I felt an enormous sense of fraternity that day.

__The Two Choirs__   Then came one of those hilarious episodes which make travel rewarding and instructive. Our factotum Moszuk had arranged far in advance that the Poznan Boys' Choir would entertain in the town hall with a special concert in our honor. This pleased me, because the choir was famous throughout Europe and had sung at the White House in Washington. But when we reached Poznan, we discovered that there were two boys' choirs, one sponsored by the Church, one by the Communist laity, and we found ourselves in the midst of a community wrangle over which choir would sing. As I listened to the arguments pro and con, I thought: "This is rather out of proportion. All I did was write a book. That's not an adequate cause for this kind of hassling. But I do want to hear those boys sing."

The impasse was resolved in a manner which still staggers me: "We will give two concerts in succession, one by the church choir, one by the other." We then filed into the audience chamber decorated in medieval style, and there stood before us on carefully prepared tiers the first choir. It consisted of some three dozen boys with angelic high voices and costumes of brown velvet jackets, white neck ruffles, tan knee-length shorts and white ribbed stockings. They were backed up by 16 men in tuxedos, who provided the necessary baritone and tenor notes.

They sang magnificently, products of a specialization that has flourished in Poznan for centuries. The sweet soprano voices of the boys were unbelievable, with two soloists who specialized in soaring notes of the greatest purity. But such notes alone might have proved somewhat monotonous had not the powerful men's voices come in to support them. The two contrasting groups formed a most enchanting mix, and as the first full-length concert ended, I wondered: "What can the next offer that will be half as good?"

I was not allowed to know which was the holy choir and which the profane. But when the second group appeared, a smaller number of boys dressed this time in red jackets, black shorts and the same white stockings, with 16 men as before in tuxedos, they sang like a choir of nightingales on a summer's eve. The men's basses were tremendous, the boys' sopranos remarkable. And as the singing stopped, much to my regret, I thought: "If anyone ever asks me: 'Jim, have you ever heard a real boys' choir perform?' I believe I'll be entitled to reply, 'Yes, on a wintry day in Poznan.' "

The Significance of a Book   But even more memorable than the choirs was my chance meeting and conversation with a young man who taught English at the local university.

"I was most eager to give my students a meaningful experience with the English language," he told me. "So when we got hold of a copy of your book *Poland* in English, we cut it into 14 parts, and each student was required to translate his or her part into the best Polish possible. They jumped at the task, partly because they were eager to find out what an outsider had to say about their country.

"When the jobs were complete, we put the parts together and found ourselves with a rather good translation of your book. I won't claim it was perfect, but we did have a novel in Polish about Poland and not only our students but many others in the university read it with pleasure.

"I personally want to thank you for having taken the trouble to write such a book. It has a meaning far beyond its mere words. It is the summary of a civilization, and the fact that it was written by a foreigner gives it double authenticity. But we did wonder how you had learned so much about our land and its heroism and foibles. How did you do it?"

I told him it was the result of reading and listening and looking and thinking, and that if he asked me now which of those components had been the most important, I would not be able to choose.

I refer to this rather unusual incident because it not only throws a bright light upon the nature of writing—the chance way in which a book can find an important audience—but more importantly because it accidently verifies what has perhaps been my most haunting experience as a writer. I was, as I have explained, a member of the board which operates the radio stations broadcasting behind the Iron Curtain. Because we have always been eager to learn whether our broadcasts reach any listeners, we interrogate anyone leaving the Soviet sphere to determine their listening habits, and on two occasions Jews coming out of Russia spoke not about the radios but about something quite different:

"Your radio helped us maintain our spirits. We listened to it whenever we found a chance. But what was even more important, someone smuggled in an English book by a man named Michener, and a group of us translated this at night into Russian, penciled in a group of notebooks. We passed these books among ourselves, hundreds and maybe even thousands of readers, until the paper wore out.

"In English the book was called *The Source.* And even though it was a reasonably well-told tale, its importance to us was something quite different. We would give it to our children and tell them: 'Look, you lazy ones, if a Gentile can write this way about our religion, and take it so seriously and with so much adoration, why can't you, a Jew, take the same trouble?' And the reading of those penciled notebooks changed lives."

I feel strongly about this aspect of writing and sometimes wonder if critics, booksellers and publishers realize the significance of what books can accomplish, and with what devotion they can be treasured. Because I wish to be specific about this and enable others to verify the Polish incident, I will write the name of the young professor who supervised this translation: Professor Krysztof Sawala, Department of English, Poznan University, Poznan, Poland. More than the medal, his report made my trip to Poland worth the effort.

__Homage to Artists__   During the gala session in the gold reception hall at the Castle, I had paid affectionate testimony to the two Polish writers who played significant roles in my life, Sienkiewicz and Reymont. On the last day of our visit someone asked: "Is there something else you'd like to do in Poland?" and I said without reflecting: "I'd like to pay my respects at the graves of Sienkiewicz, Reymont, Chopin and Jan Kiepura, if that's possible." Moszuk said: "I'll look into it," and shortly he returned with this report: "Sienkiewicz nothing. Chopin's buried in Paris. But Reymont and Kiepura, they're not far from here, and off we go . . . . after we get some flowers for their graves."

It was a snowy day and quite cold, but I had brought with me a remarkable overcoat, which was very long and made of a greenish corduroy with a big collar. When dressed in it, I looked exactly like a Soviet colonel at the siege of Stalingrad. I had the coat because I had lost my own during a visit to Toronto and had been forced to borrow one from my managing secretary, John Kings, a tall, lanky Englishman. It was in this nineteenth century-style coat that I set forth to pay my tribute to two Poles, one of whom I admired, the other of whom I had relished in a delightful way.

The cemetery, a highly formal affair, was close to the government house, and some two dozen of us marched through the cemetery to the site of Reymont's grave. I would have much preferred to go alone, for the emotions I felt were agitating. When I stood before Reymont's impressive tomb, with snow falling, I realized afresh how important this man had been to me. His great novel, *Chlopi,* had opened my eyes to the world of European writing. And after him I had read with almost equal impact the now almost forgotten Danish writer, Martin Anderson Nexø, whose powerful *Pelle the Conqueror* had introduced me to Europe's proletarian writing; and then Edward Douwes Dekker, whose *Max Havelaarr* would become an inspiration for one of my best books.

As I moved forward in the snow to place my flowers on the grave, I thought: "How indebted I am to men like you, Reymont. How deprived my life might have been without you." And I bowed my head.

The Kiepura affair was a different matter, a joyous one, really. Some months back I had taken a Caribbean cruise aboard the *Sun Viking.* Each evening, before a late dinner, friends and I spent time in a congenial small bar called the Merry Widow. Its walls were cleverly adorned with large photographs of some two dozen pairs of singers—handsome tenor, lovely soprano—who had through the decades played the roles of Prince Danilo and the Merry Widow with whom he was musically involved. It was an imaginative display and an instructive one. Nelson Eddy and Jeanette MacDonald were featured, of course, as was Richard Tauber with one of his leads, and all the other famous pairs, a few of whom I did not recognize. It was a delightful little room.

But it seemed to me that the pair who best fitted the descriptions given in the operetta were the Polish tenor Jan Kiepura and his Austrian wife, Marta Eggert. They were central European, romantic, handsome, and with the proper mix of real talent and brazen exhibitionism. I was so glad to see them again, to bask in their highly polished smiles and posturings, to hear in my imagination their splendid singing, for there had never been a better-matched couple.

I had come to know Kiepura at the once-famous Sunday night operatic concerts at the Metropolitan in New York. Then, for reasonable prices, the Met offered five or six scenes from well-loved operas, utilizing always one or two top stars but filling the ranks with the younger singers recently added to the Met. It was singing at its best, a memorable treat for younger people, and an adroit way of getting them interested in full-length opera.

Once or twice each winter the papers would announce, somewhat humorously, that again on the coming Sunday there would be Polish night at the Met, which meant that the enormously popular Jan Kiepura would be singing. This was a signal for all the Poles within a hundred miles of New york to come streaming in to hear their beloved Jan sing the role of Rodolfo or young Germont. Such nights were wild and gala.

The Met had a strict rule weekdays and Sundays— no encores—and normally this was rigidly enforced. But when Kiepura sang, he could not be stopped from coming out between the velvet curtains at the end of his performance and putting on the act of the startled little boy overwhelmed by the plaudits of his followers.

Grabbing the great curtain with one hand and bringing it about him like a robe, he would gesticulate to the audience as if to say: "You mean little old me? You mean you want me to sing again?" And by one device or another he would get the orchestra started, even though they knew they should remain silent, and he would pour out the encore he had intended to sing from the start.

I knew some of the Metropolitan people at that time and asked them: "How do you let him get away with it?" and they said: "If we didn't let him give his encore, he might lead his Poles in tearing the house down." They asked me if I'd like to meet him, and at a later concert I had the pleasure of meeting both him and Marta, and I liked

them both. After that I attended whatever concerts, musi-
cals or operas they participated in, and came to think of
them as my friends.

During World War II, when Poland was once more
involved in its death struggle with both Russia and Germany, Kiepura and Eggert produced with the aid of their
Polish friends an operetta based on Chopin's music. It
might have been called *Polonaise,* and it was a sad affair,
with an eight-man cast trying to create the impression of
two hundred blazing patriots. I saw it on the third night, I
believe, and was lucky to have done so because it closed
shortly thereafter.

After the war the Sunday nights at the Met were
discontinued, and I lost sight of Jan and Marta. What
happened to them I do not know. But aboard our *Sun
Viking* in 1988 they were very much in evidence, holding
their own against the best singers of the first half of this
century. Forever young, forever central European, forever
gay in their singing, forever attuned to their audiences,
they graced the lounge. And as I studied them, seeing only
them and not their competitors, I thought: "Oh, Jan! How I
would love to see you again, milking the audience at the
Met for one last encore. Keep singing!"

When I stood before his ornate memorial in the
special cemetery, I wanted to throw my flowers high in the
air and shout my homage to him, for he had given me
evenings of delight. I restrained myself, but I did cry to the

amazement of my listeners: "Jan! We had such good times together!" And I waved a loving farewell.

_____

__The Last Day__   On the last afternoon, the government arranged for me to give a final press conference, and it was highly political. In the very room from which Jerzy Urban delivered his attacks on the United States and fought with great vigor against my radios in Munich, I exchanged pointed questioning with some three dozen sharp interrogators. I said nothing new, but I did reiterate my convictions about writing, my affection for Poland, and my delight in the warm reception both my book and I had received during this brief but exciting visit.

We discussed Polish-American relations and world prospects, and I admitted that I was as confused as them about what was happening this year, but I conceded that I was basically an optimist and that I hoped for the best. It was an appropriate meeting to end my visit.

As I was about to leave the hall, one of the newsmen said: "Did you realize that you were occupying the same chair that Jerzy Urban uses when he gives you hell?" I asked: "How did you know I was with the radios?" and he said: "Everyone knows." I said: "Then it's a hopeful sign, isn't it, Urban and I speaking from the same chair?" They laughed, but I said: "I'm sure I'd enjoy him if we ever met. He was a valiant fighter with a sharp mind." One of the men said: "Speed the day when you do meet."

Rome

*O*ur flight from Warsaw to Rome took us through Frankfurt, from which our route was almost due south, a path that carried us close to the snow-covered Alps. As we passed almost within touching distance of the great mountains, I reviewed the many times I had visited this noble city. I first saw the Tiber and the Vatican in 1932 when, with Baedeker in hand and almost memorized, I spent a week seeking only the highlights. It was then I learned that in this richest of cities, historically speaking, one could inspect substantial remains of seven major civilizations: republican Rome, the stupendous grandeur of the mournful ruins of imperial Rome, medieval Rome, renaissance Rome, papal Rome, the pomposity of Mussolini's Rome, and modern Rome, one of the world's best-run tourist cities.

And such visual wonders! The soaring arches marking the triumphs of Caesars . . . a Forum along whose aisles senators could walk today . . . a Colosseum in which festivals—without human sacrifice—could be held tomorrow . . . churches that inspire the mind . . . a Vatican City of incredible richness . . . art museums . . . plazas that delight the eye . . . . Spanish Steps filled with young people . . . these are the manifold riches of Rome that I revisit every time I return. To me Rome was a home city, the Via Sistina my private street, the great Baths of Carcalla my gymnasium and opera house. As I shall explain, the vast Basilica of San Giovanni in Laterano is my personal church, and St. Peter's the cathedral in which I worship publicly.

I was delighted to be revisiting this familiar wonderland. But as our plane entered Italy I was not thinking of Rome's past glories but of the remarkable living man our team was about to visit. In Polish, his name is Jan Pawel Drugi. To the world he is known as Pope John Paul II. I would be delighted to see him again.

"A Great Polish Hero"   This would be our sixth meeting, for I had known him first as an inconspicuous cardinal in Krakow under the name of Karol Wojtyla *(Voy-TEE-wa)*, and how I had come to meet him threw an interesting light on Polish history. I was doing my preliminary research for my proposed novel on Polish themes, and told my advisers: "Since Poland is perhaps the most intensely Catholic nation on earth, far more so than either Italy or Spain, it's essential that I know something about the peculiar role that the religion plays here." They said: "Cardinal Wyszynski *(Vy-SHIN-ski)* is your man. He's a real hero and a damned fine churchman."

Interviews were arranged, and I saw him four times, three times in Warsaw and once in Rome. He was even more impressive than my friends had said. A tall, lean man with a hawklike visage, he was a warm and instructive host. Then in his late seventies, he seemed to trust me. I asked on one occasion: "Cardinal, on Sundays I see some 90 percent of the Polish population attending mass. Clearly, this is a gesture calculated to infuriate the Russians." He smiled and even nodded slightly, so I followed: "If the Russians withdrew, how many of your Poles would still attend mass?" and he laughed outright. "About 40 percent," he said, "like in the old days. But you can build a nation with 40 percent who sincerely believe the basics."

He also told me—with the aid of an interpreter, for he spoke no English—of years spent under a house arrest imposed by the Russians: "They were disgusted with my refusal to follow their commands." Because of his intense patriotism and willingness to sacrifice even his life in defense of his religion, he became, as his interpreter assured me: "A great Polish hero, the one we depended on in difficult times."

In all that he said, he proved himself to be a man at peace with himself, at war with oppression, and determined to keep his Poland as free as possible, even though he acknowledged that in temporal matters the Soviet Union was in control and intended to remain so.

During our third visit I wanted to ask him a group of more penetrating questions. "You will find it easier," he said, "if you go down to Krakow and talk with my colleague, Cardinal Wojtyla. He speaks English." This was the first time I heard the name that was soon to become world-famous.

As I left this congenial meeting with the primate, a street-smart Polish citizen informed me as to conditions in his homeland: "It's exactly like a movie I saw once about a small clothing manufacturer on Broadway in New York. It had a clever, smooth-talking nice guy outside keeping the firm's buyers happy, and a no-nonsense tough guy inside running the shop and seeing that it made money."

"The analogy?" I asked. He explained: "Cardinal Wyszynski in command here in Warsaw is the tough guy inside, defending the church, and is he tough! Just ask the Soviets. While Cardinal Wojtyla, down in more relaxed Krakow, is the nice guy whose job it is to keep the Russians happy without giving them too much."

"Whose job is the toughest?" I asked, and he said: "They're what you call in horseracing 'an entry.' They race together, partners in everything, and if one wins, the other wins, but whoever wins, Poland comes out ahead." Then he added: "Do not let Wojtyla's relaxed style fool you. He's tough as forged steel."

I was escorted to Krakow, Poland's southern capital

in times past, by Ed Piszek. When he led me in to see his old friend, Cardinal Wojtyla, I caught a new insight into Piszek's operations. Inspired by a love for his parents' homeland, and devoutly attached to the Catholic church, he had been wildly generous in providing funds for Polish health services, education and cultural affairs, pouring millions of dollars into projects in which he believed. While I had been aware of his generosity to lay enterprises, I had not known of his largesse to the Catholic church. In Krakow it was revealed. As a friend working in Church headquarters explained:

"When the Polish Communists, under direction from the Kremlin, refuse our cardinals funds for things our men know have to be done, your Mr. Piszek comes to their aid. When the government allows them no money with which to travel to other nations, and especially to Rome on Church business, Mr. Piszek quietly provides them with the foreign exchange they need and without which they couldn't function effectively. That's why, when he comes to Poland, both Wyszynski and Wojtyla are happy to see him, for they recognize him as both a good Catholic and a supportive friend."

The Pope-to-Be in Krakow   On this first visit to Wojtyla, Piszek led me up the stone stairway in the cardinal's solid but unpretentious palace and into the dark

(continued on page 71)

Departing from Miami. Lady Blanka Rosenstiel and one of many children in Polish dress say farewell at the airport.

Arriving in Warsaw. Stanley Moszuk, the factotum par excellence, bringing a group of beautifully costumed girls to greet us.

Poland's Prime Minister Mieczyslaw Rakowski pinning the nation's highest civilian medal on previously banned writer.

Writer with newly won medal saying a few words to the gathering of intellectuals in the great golden hall of Warsaw Castle.

Lech Walesa, minutes after his historic victory in television debate with government representative, reporting to Catholic headquarters and embracing his longtime American friend Edward J. Piszek.

Top: *The vigorous folk dancers of Lublin celebrating their visitor's arrival.*
Bottom: *The second of the world-famous Poznan's boys choirs honoring their visitor with an echoing serenade.*

The writer paying his respects at the graves of Poles to whom he was indebted. Top: The martyred priest Father Jerzy Popieluszko, murdered by the Communists. Left: The star of New York's Metropolitan Opera, Jan Kiepura. Right: Poland's Nobel Prize winning novelist Wladyslaw Reymont, whose work influenced the writer.

The writer is gratified to find so many Poles with copies of his novel to be signed. Belatedly he learns that Mr. Piszek has brought the books from America to distribute among his friends and those who had helped during the visit.

Jan Pawel Drugi, the Polish Pope John Paul II, greeting a friend who had known him years before in Krakow as Karol Wojtyla, the determined cardinal who defended Poland's interests against the Soviet Communists.

*Pope John Paul II conducting mass in his private chapel in the Vatican.
Archbishop Raymond Hunthausen of Seattle concelebrated this mass.*

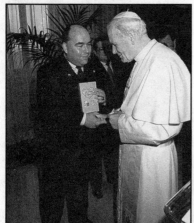

Top: *Pope John Paul with his American visitors.* Left: *Congratulating Jim Murray, originator of Ronald McDonald houses for sick children.* Bottom: *Father Wally Ziemba of Michigan is overjoyed.*

Top: *Pope John Paul greeting a close friend, Ed Piszek.*
Middle: *The pope, welcoming Larry Christensen, a former pitcher of the Philadelphia Phillies.*
Bottom: *Baseball great Stan Musial of St. Louis supervising a presentation in the pope's private chambers.*

Clockwise from top: *Atop Jesuit headquarters facing St. Peter's. The square, awaiting the pope's Sunday appearance. Stan Musial in the square. Leprechaun Jim Murray hailing a taxi. Father Ziemba in the lowest levels of St. Peter's at one of its holiest sites, the scene of martyrdom of Saints Peter and Paul.*

Sightseeing in Rome:
Top: *At the Polish Center.*
Middle: *Stan Musial, one of America's most genial men.*
Bottom: *Paying respects to the martyrs of the Colosseum.*

Stan Musial the
irrepressible. Clowning in
the Colosseum after
prayers. Playing his
harmonica for the chorale
"Tra-la-la." The woofer
dust banana.

U.S. law helping Italy fight drugs. Attorney General Dick Thornburgh.

FBI Director William Sessions. Ambassador and Mrs. Rabb hosting their gala dinner in the U.S. embassy.

Writer in Rome reflecting on the collapse of communism in Poland, Hungary and perhaps even in the Soviet Union itself.

study where the churchman waited. I remember him as a sturdy, youngish man with graying hair, not overly tall, and with a congenial, warm smile which made him look quite handsome in a rugged way. He greeted me with a firm handshake and won my wife's undying loyalty with a generous welcome, and the comment that he did not meet, here in Krakow, too many Japanese ladies. She corrected him, as she does all people who use that term, by saying proudly: "Japanese-American. I was born in the United States," and he accepted the correction.

I wish I could say that at our first meeting I perceived something magical or ethereal in the Krakow cardinal, but I didn't. In fact, during a fairly long conversation I received the distinct impression that he really had been put in place to serve as a well-behaved foil to grizzled old Wyszynski up in Warsaw, and that he, Wojtyla, was filling rather well his obligation in keeping the Soviets happy and at bay. It never occurred to me, even remotely, that this quiet-spoken, rather congenial man would have prospects outside Poland. I liked him enormously—he made you do that by his warmth and glowing eyes—but I could not differentiate him from a dozen other respectable Catholic cardinals I had known around the world. To me he was Wojtyla of Krakow, and so he would remain, I supposed. Indeed, it then seemed unlikely that he would even be named primate when Wyszynski died; his destiny was to stay in Krakow and fend off the Russians.

But as we left that first meeting, Piszek warned me: "Keep your eye on that one. He could go far." When I asked why, he said: "That one has guts of steel. He's been in the frontline battles since the age of six."

Now, as we flew past the highest Alps, I thought of the two other times I had met Wojtyla in Krakow. The first was an ordinary follow-up to the initial visit, with some hard-nosed questions about Church and state in Poland; I respected what he had to say and the statesmanlike way in which he said it. I also noted the considerable improvement in his use of English, a fact about which I complimented him. "I take lessons," he said. "To know English is important these days." I wondered if any cardinal in the other European nations was bothering to take lessons, but he added: "I take lessons in many languages." In English, his instructor could have properly awarded him an *A*.

My next visit had historic overtones, for I was now helping Piszek produce six television shows on Poland, one general overview of the nation and five fine summaries of Polish culture. As the script progressed, it became evident that what was required to give it local substance and color was a passage on the Church, and as soon as this need was voiced by the experts, I thought of Cardinal Wojtyla down in Krakow, a photogenic man in a photogenic city, and I said: "He speaks English. And I'm sure he'd look great on camera with that solid jaw and bright smile. See if he'll cooperate."

The Actor Cardinal   Because Piszek made the approach, Wojtyla agreed to the interview. We met on a warm, sunny afternoon in the cathedral gardens, where we walked together along ancient paths, coming to rest on chairs before a small wooden table where our serious conversation began. My question dealt with the relationship of a church, any church, to its civil government, any government; but from there we moved to the specific problems of a church trying to function within a society governed by Communist power. These were tough questions, but he backed off from none of them; his answers were forceful and ecumenical, addressing the great basic problems from various sides. I asked especially about the active building program whose manifestations I had seen in so many places throughout Poland: "Are you free to build churches where and when you wish?" He explained in some detail how Church and state cooperated on the rather difficult problem, for no building material would be available unless the state approved. It was, I concluded, a testy game in which each side knew what it was doing and the limits to which each could go. If the Church could not build at will, the state could not refuse all requests for permits, for then the citizens would surely protest, and the government could not risk that.

As we talked, I appreciated the delicate tightrope on which Cardinal Wojtyla danced, and I gained increased admiration for the skillful way he performed, keeping both the Vatican in Rome and the Kremlin in Moscow satisfied. This was a tough, able man with whom I was talking.

Later we eased off into less contentious questions, and now his remarkable congeniality expressed itself, for he smiled, made quiet jokes, and displayed to the world those qualities which had made him a much-loved cardinal in Krakow and the reliable right-hand man of elderly Wyszynski in Warsaw. I recalled the characterization of my Polish informant: "Smooth, easy guy outside to keep everyone happy; tough, fighting guy inside to keep things working." The Russians, I concluded, were up against a resolute pair who knew just what they wanted to do and how to do it.

We talked for about 40 minutes, during which Wojtyla revealed an almost total portrait of himself. And when we were through, with me perspiring from the strain and him at ease after a superior effort to depict himself honestly, he clasped me and asked: "How did I do? Can I land a job in Hollywood?"

When I leaned back, stunned by the question, he added with a smile: "As a young man I studied to be an actor, you know."

"You succeeded," I said.

The Surprise Election of a Pope   As the last of the pristine Alps faded into mists and our plane turned toward Rome, I recalled what I judge to have been my most unbelievable experience as a traveler, and in three-quarters of a century knocking about the world I've had quite a few. It started on a fall day in 1978. Pope John Paul I had just died, and Piszek and I had been invited to Rome to participate in several high holy masses honoring the tragic man who had occupied the papal chair for only 34 days.

I was excited by the adventure, and that excitement increased when we boarded our TWA plane in New York for the trip, for we were sharing the cabin with my long-time friend, John Cardinal Krol of Philadelphia, and three other American cardinals. I detected an air of grieving over the incredible death of John Paul I—though of course the designation of the number *I* was not yet in use—and excitement over who would be elected the dead pope's successor. The cardinals, naturally, kept their counsel to themselves, and I gleaned not even a whisper of what might eventuate at the forthcoming convocation of their College of Cardinals as they met in the Sistine Chapel for the election. I would meet with the American cardinals three times prior to the voting, and although the conversation was extensive and friendly, I was allowed to penetrate no secrets.

When we landed at Rome's Fiumicino Airport, where thieves and rascals abound, the American cardinals were whisked away in private cars while Piszek and I had to wait for clearance and the arrival of the car that would take us to the Hotel Alicorni where we had reserved rooms.

During that time we sat in the busiest part of the airport with our bags before us, and when our driver found us, we gathered our scattered gear, loaded it in and sped into Rome. But when we were finally ensconced in Ed's room, he suddenly turned ashen and said: "I must go back to the airport," and before I could ask why, he had fled.

It's quite a distance from the center of town to Fiumicino, which meant that a two-way ride would require considerable time. Exhausted by the overnight flight, I fell asleep in Ed's room and was there when he returned, with a costly black traveling case, such as executives prefer, cradled in his arms. His face was triumphant as he sat on the bed beside me. "It's a miracle. No other way to describe it."

"What's a miracle?"

"That I could leave this case unattended in that particular corridor, where everyone walked past, thousands of them, and go back almost an hour later and find it untouched."

"On the other hand, why would anyone want to steal it?"

He made no reply. Unsnapping the case, which had not been locked, he showed me that it contained $25,000 in American bills. Gravely, and with a sigh of thanks, he closed the case. Never then or since has he revealed why he had brought such funds to Rome. But once, in an entirely different setting, he did say: "I would not want my Polish cardinals to come to a major session in Rome and be at a disadvantage in comparison with others whose faithful can afford to pay their expenses."

"Don't the Polish people support their cardinals?"

"Yes. But the Communist government inspects every penny they take with them when they leave the country. They must fly Polish aircraft and pay in zloties."

"Surely they're allowed spending money for expenses here in Rome."

"They are. Zloties are no good outside Poland, so Wyszynski and Wojtyla are allowed a minimum amount of dollars, maybe $10 in all, to cover all expenses for a two-week stay in Rome."

He did not say that he had personally made up the deficiency, but in the days before the voting began he and I did visit twice with both cardinals, separately, and he did ask me to remain seated in the reception area while he talked with them privately. On the day before the College was to convene for the crucial vote, we had lunch with a subdued Wojtyla, and dinner with an exuberant Wyszynski. The latter spoke only in Polish, but I could catch the drift of his remarks. He thanked Piszek for his many gestures of friendship in years past, and me for taking the trouble to work in Poland as I had done, trying to write about the country he loved. I felt enormous affection for the old warrior that night, and told Piszek as the dinner ended: "Shame he isn't younger. He'd make a powerful pope if the warring Italians can't get their act together." The name of Wojtyla never crossed my mind.

In the days prior to voting, while I was meeting socially with the American cardinals plus one or two from other countries, we found the cardinals unwilling to say a word about the forthcoming election. But in the streets of Rome everyone was speculating on the prospects of this Italian cardinal or that. The taxi driver we had employed was a bubbling fountain of back-alley gossip: "The only reason we elected last time that pitiful fellow John Paul who just died . . . not papal material at all . . . was that the two strong men . . . either of them would make a great pope and one of them surely will next week . . ."

"What men?" I asked, and he said: "Guiseppe Cardinal Siri of Genoa and Giovanni Cardinal Benelli of Florence . . . proud men, strong men . . . they couldn't find a compromise last time, so the College settled on Luciani of Venice . . . he shocked everyone when he took the name of John Paul, first time in history a pope had two names . . . probably a bad omen . . . he wanted to ease the debate by showing that he respected both his radically different predecessors, John XXIII, the liberal, and Paul VI, the conservative."

"Have the two fighters solved their differences? It's been less than two months since their big fracas."

"You can bet they have. They'll never let a non-Italian become pope." He then surprised me by saying that his choice, and that of most of the common people, was the well-regarded Cardinal of Palermo, the charismatic Salvatore Pappalardo, much younger and livelier than the other two. "If the two biggies continue to fight, Pappalardo is certain to slip in, and he'll be a great pope."

Toward the end of the waiting period I established myself as the American barroom expert on the election: "Siri and Benelli are sure to compose their differences, and I think Siri will get it. If the fight continues, this fellow Pappalardo in Palermo is sure to be the one. He's a real comer."

"Any chance of Koening of Austria or the fellow they talk about from Argentina?"

"None whatever. The Italians will never let the papacy slip through their fingers. I think it'll be Siri, but keep an eye on Pappalardo." Once some listener said: "Pappalardo, il Papa. That sounds nice," and I realized that I too had been seduced by a euphonious name.

Appointments required that I fly home prior to the voting, and I was at my desk in Maryland on the afternoon of October 16th, 1978, when the radio announced that the new pope was to be a Polish cardinal whose name the announcer could not handle. "Wow!" I shouted, "Wyszynski made it after all!" and I was elated that they had chosen the old tiger.

But then an amazing thing happened. Phone calls began to flood in from Walter Cronkite and others with the news that the new pope was my old friend, Wojtyla, and that in all the television archives around the world there was only one substantial interview with him in English, the one I had done some years earlier in Krakow. We released it immediately, and that night I saw at least 15 rerunnings of that fine, relaxed conversation in which Wojtyla had looked so handsome and sounded so pontifical. It was an admirable introduction to a splendid man who had been such a valiant fighter in protection of his homeland and his religion, and who promised to be equally judicious and ameliorative in the papacy. When I saw the old film of him walking along with me through the cathedral gardens, I felt as if I were watching a respected friend coming to assume a position of some importance, and my heart leaped with joy for him and for the good he could do in the years ahead.

The Pope in Action   Those were the images that flooded my mind as we approached Rome in the late afternoon of December 3rd, 1988—Wyszynski saying: "Go down to Krakow and talk with Wojtyla"; my wife correcting the cardinal: "Japanese-American, born in America"; the walk through the garden; the black case with the dollars; my championing of Pappalardo; the last meetings with the two Polish cardinals prior to the voting; the exulting over his election. So I was not surprised when the agent meeting us as we deplaned informed us: "The pope says he'll have dinner with you Monday night at seven." He

was not having dinner with me, even though he was reported to have appreciated my book on Poland; he was
having dinner with Ed Piszek, who had proved his devoted
friendship through a score of years.

We saw the pope for the first time just a few minutes after we landed, for we hurried directly to the large
concert hall in which an Italian orchestra and a wonderful
choir from Krakow were giving Antonin Dvorak's *Requiem
Mass in D Major* under the direction of the young American conductor from New York, Gilbert Levine. It was a
gala, attended by thousands, and from a considerable distance we watched as the pope marched from a dais in the
middle of the hall to a podium, where he congratulated the
singers from his diocese and their American conductor. It
was a beautiful evening and launched us properly on our
visit to Rome.

Sunday morning we took our places in the great
plaza before St. Peter's to wait until noon, when the pope
would appear at his high window to bless the crowd, as
was his weekly custom. This day the square was filled with
hordes of worshippers from Catalonia in northern Spain.
They had brought with them an outstanding team of acro-
bats who set up a platform on which a group of a dozen or
more sturdy men erected a human pyramid that contained
five tiers. When the last tier was in place, high in the air, a
frail boy not over ten years old climbed up the bodies as if
they were inanimate pillars. He clambered to the very top,

crawled onto the heads of the young men there, and paused to wave to the pope before starting down. He slid gracefully from one body to the next until he, and then the others behind him, had reached the platform. The pope, who had interrupted his homily to watch the amazing performance, applauded.

He appeared, as always, at a window on one of the high floors of the Vatican, and seemed from where we stood not much more than a white-garbed speck. When he finished his words of good cheer, the bulk of them in Spanish, which he spoke easily, a group of Catalonian men automatically began a ritual which I had often seen them perform on the porch of their Barcelona cathedral as mass ended: Standing in a solemn row, arms linked, they danced a measure which began in a great solemnity, then swiftly escalated to a wild, swinging exhibition of robust liveliness. It was very Spanish, and with the red and yellow flags of that country waving at many spots in the throng, it brought the Pope's weekly Angelus meeting to a hectic conclusion.

Mass in St. Stanislaus   On Monday morning our group celebrated mass in St. Stanislaus, the Polish church not far from the Vatican. It is a lovely, small gathering place, remarkable for the severe balance maintained throughout the building. If a pillar appeared on the right, you could guarantee that a matching mate would stand on the left; and the effect was so harmonious and classically proper, that I was enchanted by the effort that had been spent in establishing and maintaining this symmetry. Mass was led by our own Father Ziemba, who introduced me to two innovations. The first was that at one point he invited each of his listeners to speak of some concern about which the listener sought guidance or confirmation, and the men spoke with great fervor, as if it were they who were conducting the mass and not their priest. I said later: "Sounds just like a Quaker meeting, where men and women in the congregation serve as their own priests," but my comments were not applauded. At my first experience with the new custom I did not speak. But on the next day, in another church with another priest, I said: "I think we can all give thanks that the potential uprising of the military in Argentina has subsided and that democracy is free once more to stumble forward." It was a prayer really, and it was answered, for the time being.

The other unfamiliar development, from the days when I attended rigorous masses in Glasgow, where Catholics were on the defensive, came when the worshippers were invited to move about and shake hands with everyone within reach. Since I was enjoying myself enormously with the individuals in my gang, I found this easy and rewarding. I found myself embarrassed, however, when Father Ziemba offered communion to his group. As a Quaker, I had never participated in this rite; to me it was totally strange and even debatable, so I refrained when the wafer was offered. Father Wally, an ecumenical type, accepted my action in good spirit, and no one else referred to it.

Dinner with the Pope   On Monday night, Ed Piszek, Stan Musial and I dressed in our dark suits, got into our car along with Domenico del Vecchio, who would show us the way, and drove the short distance from our hotel to the Vatican. We entered the Vatican walls at the designated place, and drove through that myriad of narrow alleyways and through one stone portico after another, until we stopped in a small square. There, an inconspicuous door led us into the ground floor of the papal quarters, where an almost hidden door took us to a small elevator. It was tended by an old friend, Monsignor Stanislao Dziwisz (*JEE-vish*), who had worked with the pope since the early days in Krakow. Greeting us warmly, he said: "The Holy Father is looking forward to dining with you."

He took us to an upper floor, where we waited in an austerely decorated room containing a handsome antique table, round in form and decorated with inlaid classical figures. On it rested a copy of my novel *Poland,* so prominently displayed that I grew embarrassed looking at it and would have turned it over if possible, except that from the back cover glared my big face.

We talked quietly among ourselves until a flurry of feet in the corridor alerted us to the pope's approach.

Bursting into the room as if he were happy to see us again, he went immediately to Piszek and embraced him. Then he came to me with a warm greeting, and without being aware of what I was doing, I said: "I am so glad to see you, my dear friend." That unusual phrase would be repeated twice later, but not by me.

We then turned to the novel, which had been the occasion of our meeting, and he said briefly that it had accomplished much good, and the matter was dropped.

In the meantime, one of the most adept and skillful photographers, regularly employed by the Vatican, was circulating and snapping at a rate that dazzled. Without my being aware of his presence, he would, within less than a minute, catch six fine photographs of the pope examining the novel and then, before we could speak to him, the man was gone with dozens of photographs of our group. It was breathtaking.

We then passed into the dining room. It was a table for seven: the pope on one side, his two aides at the ends, and we four facing him. No photographs were allowed in this room, and I assumed that the priests were present to protect him from any improper report of the off-the-record meeting that one of us might later give the press. I have experienced this sensible precaution with various heads of state.

This would be my third meeting with His Holiness. The first came shortly after his election and involved only Piszek and me; we talked that time with extra-ordinary frankness about his new job, and had I been a reporter my accent would have made headlines around the world. I can say that he asked me about how to deal with the press, and asked Piszek what tricks he had learned to make travel easier. Mostly we laughed, robust peasant laughter, for we all came from ordinary, almost peasant stock.

The second discussion came a year or so later when others were present, and this time we talked almost exclusively about sports: skiing, soccer, mountain climbing, with him participating vigorously. In none of my conversations, not even in Krakow, did we discuss anything pertaining to theology or the inner governance of the Church. In later years I would say: "I love the pope for his humanity, his wit and his keen sense of social justice; I sometimes find his severe conservatism on doctrine difficult to appreciate in this modern world." I did not know it as we sat down to dinner, but I would within a few hours be thrust into the middle of the dilemma I had so succinctly described.

The meal consisted of three courses served by a nun: some of the best cannelloni I have ever had; an excellent chicken dish; and, I feel sure, some kind of dessert; but I was so busy listening that I took no specific notice of it. The pope ate none of this; he had soup with crackers and a plate of fruit.

This night his conversation was totally different from the two times before. He was older now, well tempered by the fires in which he had participated, including the attempt on his life, and the struggles with a renegade movement in France, the Cologne protest organized by the German cardinals, not to mention the uneasiness many American priests and scholars felt about his intrusion into their educational patterns. No country jokes this time, no chitchat about games, only the thoughtful reflections of a great man grappling with worldwide problems. On two different occasions he looked across the table at me and said: "So you are the man who called me his friend," and I could not tell whether this was a rejection of what he had deemed an unwarranted familiarity or simply a reflection of an unusual greeting. But I did get the feeling that at his second repetition there was a sharp edge to his voice.

I could not be mistaken, of course, when he rebuked me for something I said about the present dictator, General Wojciech Jaruzelski. We were talking about the novel, and I said: "Its remarkable record was due in part to the three lucky accidents which thrust Poland onto the front pages. Your election to the papacy made everyone snap to attention, Lech Walesa's bold moves attracted applause, and General Jaruzelski's imposition of martial law focused sharp attention on Poland. I had not anticipated any one of these events, but I had known that something would have to happen."

When he looked at me quizzically, I made bold to explain my last point: "In the late summer and early autumn of 1981 I traveled to almost every corner of Poland, and wherever I went I found the hotels and restaurants with almost no food. We really went hungry. No goods in the stores, and in early October when I was far south on the old Hungarian border at Krynica I saw real poverty. Believe me, Poland was ready to explode, and I left during the second week in October fully expecting the Russian tanks to be in Warsaw before Christmas. That this did not happen was a miracle, and I give thanks."

He looked at me harshly as I said this, and in the silence I continued: "So in the years that followed, I never spoke poorly of Jaruzelski, for although I was aware of the wrong things he had done, I was also aware of what the alternative could have been, and I was grateful that both Russia and Poland drew back from what would surely have proved a bloody confrontation, worse than Hungary or Czechoslovakia."

He said nothing, and the matter was dropped, but I had the feeling that there was much he might have wanted to say. When he spoke again, he surprised us all: "I welcome you to my private mass at seven tomorrow morning, here in the Vatican." The evening meal was over.

A Papal Mass   Next morning at 5:30 our entire team of nine was up early. We dressed in blue suits to travel to a new part of St. Peter's, where a huge bronze door awaited us. There, in a sloping areaway, waited some two dozen civilians plus a cadre of priests from various parts of the world who would assist him in the solemn rite of a papal mass. We ascended to the chapel by six or seven flights of the longest marble stairs I have seen or attempted to climb. "Stairway to heaven," someone in our group whispered, but Piszek described it more accurately as the "cardiac climb." With my weak left leg I like to climb up stairs for exercise, so I had a frolic, but two days later muscles not used previously were painfully sore.

The climb was worth it, for we were led to a handsome library where others who would participate in the mass were assembling. They were mostly priests, and two of the younger ones recognized Stan Musial and crowded in to pepper him with questions about baseball. "I'm entitled to be here," he told them, "because I'm also a Cardinal." This play on words delighted them.

However, I noticed among the younger priests one who stood beside an older man in the colorful habit of an archbishop, and I could tell that they were speaking of me. Finally they crossed the room, and the younger man asked: "Are you James Michener, the writer? They told us you might be here this morning." When I nodded, the young man said: "The archbishop wanted to meet you," and the older man stuck out his hand: "I'm Raymond Hunthausen from Seattle. We heard you'd been working in Alaska."

In that instant the early morning mass with the pope became not only an extraordinary religious service but also a profound personal revelation. For after Hunthausen—a controversial figure, temporarily removed from his post by the pope—and I had shaken hands, I said in an explosion of emotion: "Archbishop, it's providential that you and I should meet here in these circumstances." Before he could ask why, I rushed ahead: "When I published my novel on Poland I was abused and excoriated, just as you were last year. But the other day the government invited me back, said their judgment had been hasty, and bestowed their highest honor on me in reward for the good work I had done for their country. They don't like me any more now than then, but they did welcome me as an honest man."

I think tears came to Hunthausen's eyes, but I did not wait for him to speak. "With you, it's obviously been the same," I continued. "You took some hard knocks, were humiliated in public, practically defrocked, and today I meet you here at dawn. Clearly the Holy Father has invited you to Rome, and now you're to help him officiate at his private mass. How much more can he do to heal the breach?"

"After the mass I'm to have breakfast with him . . . at his insistence," said Hunthausen.

It is difficult to describe the passion that flowed between us at that moment. We were both older men. We'd been through a lot. We'd kept our mouths shut, taken whatever was thrown, and had remained silent when it would have been so easy to fight back. And now our circles had come full closed, and we stood together in a most unlikely spot at a most unlikely moment. But I was still the garrulous one: "Father Hunthausen, I'm overwhelmed by the coincidences, and I'm prouder of the pope for his actions this day than I have ever been before. It's the right thing he's doing, and it's the proper way to do it. I shall join in the mass with a full heart. I'm so glad you spoke, I'm really so glad."

The pope's private chapel was a gorgeous affair, with plain white marble walls accented by a tessellated floor, a simple altar and a handsome pair of paintings depicting the executions of Saints Peter and Paul. Some dozen priests assisted in the service, but at the pope's right hand sat Archbishop Hunthausen in his white robes and red cap. What was going through his mind I could not guess.

Contrary to recent changes in conducting the mass, John Paul II continues the old pattern, with his back to the congregation and his face toward the farthest wall, which formed a kind of secondary altar. I was unprepared for this particular mass, for although I had become familiar with the rite, especially since I had been attending one a day on this trip, I was unaware that a priest officiating could, at his will, spend long spells in silent prayer; and the pope's silences were so protracted that once again I felt as if I were back in a Quaker meeting, where occasionally the silence is unbroken for a full 60 minutes.

There was an unexpected moment that produced great happiness for our group. Father Ziemba had asked the pope's aide, Father Dziwisz, if our Irish tenor, Tom O'Leary, could sing "Ave Maria" during the mass, and had been told: "Impossible." But when the important part of the mass ended, Ziemba considered himself free to signal Tom to start singing. As he explained it later: "He said Tom couldn't sing during the mass, but I didn't ask about after." The pope must have been astonished as he knelt praying while behind him came the liquid, lovely voice of O'Leary singing the great Bach-Gounod anthem. It was a magnificent moment. I was standing beside the two men when the mass ended and the pope told Tom: "That was lovely singing. Thank you."

I forget now at what point in the long service—we were in chapel for more than an hour—the taking of Communion came, but the pope himself administered it, with the aid of Hunthausen and another, and for the first time in my life I joined the faithful in moving forward to accept the wafer from the hands of Jan Pawel Drugi, who had played such an important though accidental role in my work on Poland.

When the mass ended, everyone reassembled in the room in which I had met Hunthausen at the start, and the pope moved among us, exchanging greetings and allowing himself to be photographed with worshippers who had come from afar, especially four tiny nuns from Vietnam. When he came to our group he posed with each of us in turn, and here for the first time he joked and exchanged pleasantries as if he were a parish priest at the close of prayer. Grasping my hand in both of his, he said: "Keep writing those long books," and he crossed the room to where Archbishop Hunthausen awaited, threw his arm about him and led him in to breakfast.

Students from America   The bright warm days that followed constituted the kind of introduction to Catholic Rome that visiting Protestants would rarely see. I was invited to the Pontifical Holy Mass held in the sumptuous Chapel of the North American College, where top students from American seminaries come for four years to finish their studies for the priesthood. The mass was conducted by Joseph Cardinal Bernardin, visiting from Chicago, a powerful voice in the Church, and featured an extended sermon by an American priest with no special title or dress named Father Ray Brown. When he started talking, I assumed that he was some functionary handed the job so that he could later boast to his friends that he had participated in a mass conducted by Bernardin, but as his homily rolled on and on, I became fascinated by the rare quality of the man's organizational and expository gifts. He preached in the old style of nineteenth-century orators, and three times when he came to a kind of peroration on a given topic, I muttered: "Here we end," but then he launched into the exploration of some collateral subject more brilliantly than before, and I listened with awe.

I did not time him, but since the entire mass consumed an hour and 45 minutes, he must have spoken for at least an hour. And since I listened closely to his almost magical flow of words, I caught the sharp rebuke he handed my favorite, Archbishop Hunthausen. Without mentioning him by name, he put him and all other near-heretics into their place, for he said that the mere exploration of enticing ideas without solid founding in the basic truths of Catholicism was futile and to be condemned . . . or something along that line. When he finished, a priest I did not know whispered: "He's our church's supreme authority on scripture. He spoke so long because he will want to put his message into print. In that form it will circle the world and become its own dogma."

At the lunch that followed, with nearly a thousand listeners as hungry as me, good fortune placed me in the position of honor next to a valued acquaintance, William Cardinal Baum, formerly of Washington but now serving in the Vatican as head of all Catholic education. I had talked with him during the interregnum between the two John Pauls and found him amazingly judicious, informed and skilled in conciliating diverse views. I asked him: "Of a hundred of these young men studying in Rome today, how many will become bishops?" and he replied: "We hope that most of them will. They've been picked as winners." I then asked: "How do you ensure that the Church as a whole gets the proper mix of charismatic leaders and solid but not so dramatic scholars?" He clapped his hands and said: "Now that's our perpetual problem. At times, in the United States at least, it seems to run all in one direction, but then corrective steps are taken."

"So you do get a safe supply of the scholars you need?" I asked. And he replied: "You heard one today. Ray Brown is one of our best, and he'll stay with that job, providing us all with illumination."

A Bizarre Performance   This was, as I have already demonstrated, to be a fortnight of bizarre coincidences, and now came one of the strangest. Sitting across from Baum was a tall, smiling bishop with a naughty smile, as if he heard jokes denied to others, and when he learned that I was busy working on a novel on the Caribbean, he said teasingly: "I'll wager you'll miss one of the most important factors of all." And I replied: "I always do, and it angers me. What's it this time?"

"Cricket," he said. "The West Indies lives on cricket, and you Americans never seem to catch on to that fact."

Entering the spirit of his game, I used a pompous phrase: "My good man, not long ago I spent an entire afternoon with Sir Gary Sobers learning the secrets of a chinaman."

"Now what can that be?" a priest asked, and I explained: "A left-handed googly," at which the table exploded.

Bishop Kennedy, my first interrogator and director of the English College in Rome, then took over and explained that a googly was a tantalizing form of bowling in which the ball took unexpected twists and turns, knocking down the wicket and dismissing the batter. Rising to full height, he demonstrated the normal googly, thrown with the right arm, and then revealed that he had thrown his with the left, which made his a chinaman: "Very deadly, the chinaman," and with him and me standing beside Cardinal Baum, he demonstrated how he had manipulated his arm to achieve the proper googly twist.

He then asked me how I knew so much about cricket. I said that I had always admired Sir Gary, one of the black West Indians to be knighted for his rare skill, but that I was also familiar with the immortal Three W's of island cricket: Worrell, Weekes and Walcott, who had torn English teams apart in the 1950s and 1960s. "You're qualified to write about the Caribbean," he said, and I thought: "How strange to get my diploma from a Catholic bishop in Rome."

__A Visit with the Jesuits__   Archbishop John Foley, a priest I had known favorably in Philadelphia, was now serving in Rome as director of Vatican communications, and because I had been attentive to his Philadelphia superior, Cardinal Krol, he sent a message to our hotel: "I would like to conduct a mass in honor of Mr. Michener in the crypt of St. Peter's." So, early on our last full day in the city, we entered the vast cathedral and descended into its bowels, where popes of great distinction lay buried and where a tiny, handsome chapel stands over the supposed but fairly well-documented burial site of St. Peter. It was a solemn mass, far from the normal crowds, and I appreciated Foley's thoughtfulness in inviting me to participate.

The Catholic portion of the visit to Rome ended on a somber note, for Father John O'Brien, a gregarious Canadian Jesuit supervising the worldwide educational work done by that order, invited us to a special mass held in one of the chapels in Jesuit headquarters, and visiting those halls again was a bittersweet experience. On the one hand, I was pleased to see once more where this powerful order headquartered, for I admired Jesuit education as I had observed it in American schools like Georgetown, Fordham, St. Louis University, Boston College and Loyola in New Orleans; on the other, I was distressed to learn that on a bed in the building lay immobilized the aging lion who had once headed the Jesuits, Father General Pedro Arupe. He had been a powerful force in Jesuit affairs in the Church, so powerful indeed that he had run afoul of the hierarchy.

I had dined with him twice in the high days of his command. We had met in this building, and had talked together of the various sites about the world in which we had labored, he far more widely than I. And I had thought as I listened: "Arupe and Lowell Thomas, the only two men I've met who've been more places than I." I liked his feisty style and his far-ranging plans for the future, and at the conclusion of each visit we wished each other good fortune on our future travels.

Alas, he and his Jesuits became so powerful and so self-directed that when John Paul II assumed command in the Vatican, one of the first moves he made was to bring the fractious Jesuits back under strict papal control. In one sense that was a curious move, because Ignatius Loyola, a most difficult man from the Basque region of Spain, had in 1539 to 1540 initiated his religious-military order to serve as the right hand of the pope. But most of its superiors-general had been like Arupe: strong-minded, determined and often galloping off on missions of their own. Instead of defending the pope, they were often at war with him in doctrinal and managerial matters.

In my research on various national histories I came repeatedly on paragraphs like this, and it could pertain to many different countries:

*In 1641 the civil and clerical powers alike could
tolerate the Jesuit interference no longer, so with
eager assistance from Rome they banished the Order
forever from the country, and there was weeping and
recrimination when the Jesuits departed. Of course, in
1683 when all was in disarray the Jesuits were
invited back, and swiftly they resumed control in the
same arrogant manner, so that in 1703 they had to
be expelled again. But of course in 1749 they were
again welcomed.*

The various expulsions of Jesuits from one nation
or another must mount into the hundreds, and almost
always they were welcomed back because citizens recognized that they were needed to run the schools, the missions and other civilizing agencies. I am certain that had I
at some time in the past been Catholic, I would have been a
Jesuit.

At the height of his power, Father General Arupe
was demoted, to be replaced by a much more sober leader
and one who would take direction from the new Pope:
Peter-Hans Kolvenbach, a Dutchman with a stable reputation. Tall and slim, with a distinguishing mustache and
closely trimmed goatee, he has assumed quiet command of
the Jesuits while maintaining a low profile, a contrast to
Arupe's style. A former missionary with long experience in
the field, he is expected to establish order among his

priests, but I can visualize the church histories of 2050 writing:

"After half a century of relative quiescence, in 2037 the Jesuits again found themselves with a charismatic leader who led them joyously into battle."

In the meantime Father Arupe lay dying in the small room directly above the chapel in which we held our mass with Father O'Brien. A young priest told us: "Father Arupe lies up there unable to move or speak, but we know that he does hear. If you sing today, sing loud." Tom O'Leary did sing a beautiful hymn, and powerfully. I hope Arupe heard it.

Two Treasured Churches   I had often assured inquiring friends: "I'd convert to Catholicism if two minor requirements could be met. First, I'd want to be one of the American cardinals, not because of vanity or love of high office but because every cardinal throughout the world is assigned a home church in Rome for which he is spiritually responsible and on which is based his right to be a cardinal. Second, I would want my Roman church to be one of the original basilicas from the time of Constantine the Great, A.D. 306 to 337, because those two churches are among the most treasured in Christian history and are thus reserved for the highest symbolism of the Catholic church. I feel a profound identification with each: Maggiore, founded in 332, because of its almost heavenly form and style, a Renaissance masterpiece with ornate chapels that delight the eye; San Giovanni Laterano because of its ancient simplicity, great barnlike austerity, and overall sensation of being a part of the very oldest aspects of Christianity."

On any visit I make to Rome, I pay my respects to these two great churches, for I feel them to be a signal part of my heritage. When they were built, Protestantism had not yet broken away from Rome. Had I lived in those days Maggiore and Laterano would have been my churches. I still feel as if I own part of them, and if continued affection bestows ownership, as in many cases it does, then I truly am part owner of these great and ancient buildings.

I often wonder which of the two I prefer, and my love of art impels me strongly toward Maggiore, for in all respects it is more artful than Laterano. But whenever I walk along that quiet Roman street leading from Maggiore to the older edifice and I see peeking beneath the arching branches the rude outline of San Giovanni, I think: "That's my kind of church. Four-square, no nonsense, a huge sprawling thing, built by artisans inspired by powerful emotions and a desire to build something big to pay honor to the spirit that drove them. A church like this calls to me, and when I stand before the tall plain doors and enter into that vast internal space I am once more awed by the vision of men who, in the early days of Christianity, could have imagined and then built a church of such dimension."

No French cathedral, no perfect English one like

Salisbury or Winchester, or little gem like Sacre-Coeur in Paris, creeps inside my soul the way Laterano does. It speaks to me, and when I stand inside its far-reaching vistas I imagine myself the cardinal from Detroit or San Diego responsible for its continued well-being.

American Politics   Before we landed in Rome on that first Saturday afternoon prior to the Dvorak *Requiem,* I told our group: "Since I am, in a sense, an officer of the government because of the radio thing, I think we ought to do something I rarely do. Inform our ambassador to Italy that we're in town and would like to pay our respects." When the others approved, I was asked: "By the way, who is our ambassador?" Someone said: "Chap named Robb." The only Robb I could think of was one I knew, Chuck Robb, Lyndon Johnson's son-in-law. "But I believe he was just elected to the Senate," I said.

Since no one could solve the impasse, we agreed that we would call upon the ambassador and present our credentials in the way British citizens do when traveling abroad. A phone call was made. We were invited to speak with the ambassador at ten next morning, and in that simple gesture we found ourselves catapulted into a diplomatic brouhaha that seemed in time to involve much of Rome. Because when we marched in, all nine of us to pay our respects, I heard a friendly shout: "Michener! What are you doing in Rome?" and an old friend from Tokyo days

rushed forward to embrace me. It was Maxwell Rabb, who
had held the post in Rome for the past eight years, and with
the announced retirement of Mike Mansfield from Japan
he would become the United States' longest-serving ambassador.

It was a joyous reunion, filled with endless laughs
about the old days and reminiscences of almost forgotten
friends and rascals. Few foreign capitals provided a cast of
characters like Tokyo in those early days of the occupa-
tion: MacArthur, his Prussian aide Willoughby, Hirohito,
Maggie Higgins and her reporter adversary Homer Bigart,
Marilyn Monroe, Syngman Rhee over in Korea, and notable diplomats and newsmen galore. Rabb had been a
prudent operator in those hectic days, and I was delighted
to renew his acquaintance, for he and his wife Ruth were
first-class hosts.

I had expected us to make a brief, pro forma report
of our recent travels and our dinner with the pope, but that
proved to be far from adequate, for without prior planning
Rabb blurted out: "Say, Michener, we're having a cocktail
party this evening for a powerful traveling committee from
Washington. Appointments in the new administration and
all that. I'm sure they'd like to meet you and Stan Musial, so
I want your entire group to come over to the residency at
seven. Lots of drinks and hors d'oeuvres, but no sit-down.
That's reserved for the committee." Consulting among
ourselves, we said: "We'll be there," and as we walked to

the door of the embassy, Rabb said: "The residency is worth seeing. A palace set down in a majestic garden." Then he added: "Members of this committee could be important to us. You'll add a flair."

Although I was not aware of it at the time, the people managing our tour had already been in touch with our other ambassador to Rome, the one accredited to the Vatican, and since he was a close friend of mine, he had told them: "I'd love to see Michener again. We'll have a reception and dinner Friday night."

A Trusted Friend   Ambassador Frank Shakespeare, a fighting red-haired Irishman more conservative than Attila the Hun, had been a media maven whose first job in government was as director of the United States Information Service (USIS), as it was then called. Because the law required him to have at least one Democrat on his advisory board, he chose me as someone he could work with, even though we were miles apart in our philosophies. I had found him reliable, intelligent, a good man where political infighting was concerned, and passionately devoted to the American way of life as opposed to communism. For five years I had helped him fight our nation's propaganda battles abroad, and when he moved from USIS to take operating control of our radio broadcasting to the Soviet Union and the Iron Curtain block, he invited me to accompany him. We had long years together in the war of ideas, and although we differed widely in our view of internal American politics, we had almost identical views about our problems abroad. There was one significant difference: A friend said of Frank, "He'd like to bomb the Kremlin tomorrow"; I was for long-range conciliation, what one might have termed "glasnost before its time."

After our stint together in the propaganda wars, he had moved on to become our ambassador to Portugal, and from there had leapfrogged into the highly desirable post at the Vatican. As a devoted Catholic, he relished the latter assignment.

I was eager to see him for another reason other than friendship. I had been dismayed a year ago when newspapers broke the story, with screaming headlines, that Shakespeare had been Lieutenant Colonel Oliver North's point man in Europe, had served as a conduit in various enterprises, and had provided North with intelligence secrets. When the story broke, I had wanted to ask him about this, but decided not to do so by mail. At the Friday night dinner at his quarters I would have a chance to get some explanations. I could believe that he was ideologue enough to support North's clandestine operations, but doubted that he would be so foolish as to do so while serving as an ambassador and keeping the State Department in ignorance of his deeds.

In the meantime, we put on our best suits and reported to Ambassador Rabb's imperial residency—the

United States had picked it, not Rabb—and there we saw international diplomacy at its most glamorous. The vast estate, almost in the middle of Rome, had belonged to an important Italian family, and now provided spacious gardens, glittering halls, quiet rooms, a banquet area, and exquisite decorations. It was filled this night with Italian leaders, Americans stationed permanently in Rome, the visiting American leaders, and us nine stragglers. It was to be a gala evening.

Veteran of the Wars   As I approached the reception line where the ambassador stood with the visiting delegation, I heard my name called, and there stood a man with whom I had fought the political wars in Pennsylvania, Richard Thornburgh, former governor of that state and now Attorney General of the United States. We had served together in the notable Pennsylvania Constitutional Convention, which had enabled our state to be the only major one to bring its antiquated basic law into order for the twenty-first century. All other major states had failed, Texas, New York and Maryland conspicuously; we had succeeded because sensible Republicans like Bill Scranton and Thornburgh had cooperated with us Democrats to complete a splendid job. I had great respect for this man, and had stayed with him in the gubernatorial mansion when he arranged for the state to award me a medal for my writing.

The evening had solemn overtones, because Thornburgh had brought with him Judge William Sessions, newly appointed director of the FBI and therefore an associate of Thornburgh's. The two men spoke movingly of their mission to Italy—an attempt to control the international movement of drugs—and convinced the guests that they meant business. But then the tension relaxed as Thornburgh, remembering his years as governor of Pennsylvania, invited two of his former constituents, Stan Musial and me, to stand beside him and give short talks, which Stan did with such a light touch that he won the hearts of everyone. Ambassador Rabb was so pleased with Stan's performance that he cried impulsively: "You were such a hit, Stan, that you and Michener must bring your whole team here tomorrow for a festive lunch." I said that nine was a mite large for such an affair, but Rabb said: "That's what we have the mansion for."

It was one of the finest embassy lunches I have ever attended. The day was warm. Sunlight filled the gardens. The talk was lively. Some good stories were thrown about, and as it ended, Rabb astonished me by saying privately: "Jim, on Friday a very powerful congressional committee is flying in for an inspection. House Appropriations, and they are crucial to State Department operations abroad. I'm giving a dinner for them Friday night, and to give it a touch of class, I want you and Stan Musial to attend, just as you did last night."

I said: "I think something has been arranged at Frank Shakespeare's," and he said: "That's no problem. The others go to Frank's, you and Stan come here. It's very important, Jim, that you and Stan be here."

I said: "I'll check it out, but I'm afraid it's all been arranged." The lovely luncheon ended with me in such a quandary that when we returned to the daily strategy sessions in our hotel I warned the men: "This cannot end well. Beware."

From there on things began to fall apart so totally that I said: "The only one capable of handling this is the fellow who writes the French bedroom farces." But I also laid down the base decision from which I would not be dislodged: "My obligation is to Shakespeare and I cannot violate it. He'd kill me."

Members of the House Appropriations Subcommittee on State Department Affairs did arrive. They looked into everything relating to the Rome embassy and satisfied themselves that Rabb was doing a good job. When they heard that Stan Musial was in town they cried: "Can we meet him? We used to watch him play." Also, several of the wives asked if I too might be available: "We love his books."

Thus confirmed in his suspicion that Musial might lend adornment to his gala dinner, Rabb then issued an order: "My car will be at your hotel at seven and will bring Musial and Michener to the residency for the big dinner."

When our manager pointed out that Ed Piszek was head of our delegation, Rabb said: "Bring him too." When I asked: "What about Frank Shakespeare?" I was told: "That's all been settled. The rest go there."

Voices from the Past   What I have to say next seems preposterous, but if you check the *International Herald Tribune* for Friday, December 8, 1988, you will find an article that stunned me. It was by Anthony Lewis of the *New York Times* and dealt with four instances in which Colonel Oliver North had enthusiastically cited various authorities, including Rabb and Shakespeare, as having either condoned or supported his ventures. But each of the authorities cited had denied ever having spoken to North, or, in several of the cases, even having met him or known about him. When North claimed that Maxwell Rabb, our ambassador to Italy, had telephoned him to congratulate him on the capture of the *Achille Lauro* murderers of the crippled American, Rabb asked: "Who is Oliver North?" So both of my ambassadors had been involved with North, and I was eager to know to what extent.

The evening, as I had predicted, turned into complete chaos. Ambassador Rabb's car did arrive to whisk Stan Musial, Piszek and me to Rabb's mansion, where we met the delightful, savvy, crusty longtime members of the House Appropriations Subcommittee. A lavish sit-down dinner was underway in great style, and I sat at a table with four congressmen, each of whom had been reelected so many times that he had bulletproof seniority. At another table, Musial kept the crowd enthralled with tales of his years as one of baseball's major stars, and Piszek held sway at his own table filled with politicians.

But in the middle of the dinner we received urgent phone calls from the other ambassador: "Where are my guests?" and Rabb made a hasty Solomonic decision: "Send cars over there and bring everyone over here. We'll set up two more tables."

This move was underway when Shakespeare appeared, rather shaken, for his evening was being snatched from him. The congressmen, however, sided with Rabb and felt that one big festivity was just what was needed, and it looked as if everyone would revel at the mansion.

But then a voice of common sense intervened. Shakespeare was called to the phone on which his daughter, who served as his hostess in Rome, was laying down the law in such unmistakable terms that our driver later reported: "I could hear her screaming across the room. It was so painful I left."

She pointed out that she had food prepared and servants waiting to serve it, and she expected her father, Stan Musial, Ed Piszek, Jim Michener and everyone else in our party to be there within ten minutes. I saw Shakespeare as he left the phone, ashen: "Maxwell, my good friend, I've got to go and take my guests with me. Orders."

Rabb was both understanding and gracious. Tapping me on the shoulder just as the four congressmen and I were getting down to business he said: "Sorry. Jim's been called elsewhere."

Through the lovely Roman night we sped past great houses, down narrow streets, alongside famous churches including Maggiore, close to the pillars of St. Peter's, and up to America's second embassy in Rome. It was a riotous evening, good food, endless nonsense, singing and the fellowship that comes at the end of a long journey. Never was Stan Musial funnier.

He showed us first his famous "cutting the banana" trick in which a banana with its skin intact is sliced into four cleanly cut segments by a knife which never touches the banana. "This is possible only because I sprinkle the knife with invisible woofer dust imported from Australia, at great expense, I may say." Scattering the invisible dust and waving his knife, he handed the banana to a watcher. "Peel it part way." When the helper did, he revealed the banana neatly sliced at that point. Continuing to unpeel the fruit, the man showed us the next slice and finally the last one. Skin untouched, knife only in the air, never near the banana, the magic woofer dust from Australia had turned the trick.

He also did a fantastic trick with a huge mirror which was so improbable that the three priests who had joined our group exploded with laughter and disbelief. But the part I liked best was when he took out his German harmonica and led us in group singing: "It's a simple tune but the words are very tricky. Pay close attention and see if you can master them." They were "Tra-la-la, la-la, la-la, la-la," repeated four times. "Now the second verse." Same words. Then with enormous enthusiasm and pleading: "Let's see if we can do the third verse." Same words with his leaping frenetically all over the place as he played his music.

I halted the nonsense by asking Tom O'Leary to sing one of the greatest of the Christmas carols, the French "Cantique de Noël." At the conclusion I stood beside Tom to recite the moving words of the second verse:

Truly he taught us to love one another
His law is love and his gospel is peace.
Chains shall be broke for the slave is our brother
And at his coming oppression shall cease.

Then Tom soared into the wonderful conclusion: "O night divine! O night when Christ was born," and we felt that Christmas was near.

When I returned to my seat I whispered to Shakespeare: "Have you seen today's *Tribune*? Big story about Maxwell Rabb and Oliver North."

The words produced the effect of an exploding land mine: "North! Don't speak to me about North! That name almost destroyed me," and in seething anger he ran to his study and brought back a thick file of newspaper clippings. Bold headlines revealed that he had been North's agent in

Portugal and that he had helped in some diverse ways to speed the colonel's various strategies. The stories were even worse than the one I had seen fleetingly.

"How did you get trapped in an operation like that?" I asked, with the frankness to which an old friend was entitled.

"Jim! These entire stories, every one of them, a pack of lies. I never spoke to North, never served as his conduit for information, military goods or money. Not a word is true." And he showed me the spade-work an acquaintance of mine, the notable Washington lawyer Leonard Garment, had done in tracking down the lies, exposing them and clearing Frank's name unconditionally.

In fairness to North it must be said that the newspaper stories did not implicate him in disseminating charges against Shakespeare; they originated, apparently, with an unnamed source in Nicaragua, but who he was, his nationality or his association with North was not revealed.

"Then the whole thing was fake?" I asked in the presence of all.

"Every word. They could just as easily have said it was you. I had no involvement whatever." And although the broken evening allowed me no opportunity to question Max Rabb, I feel sure that he would have said the same.

The Circles of Life   I have reported rather fully on my unpremeditated excursion to cities and people I have held in high regard because I wanted to demonstrate how a writer reacts to certain recurring artistic factors. I have always been convinced that human life, and that of societies, too, moves in great circles, and that in time we come back to our beginnings. Poland accepted me, Poland rejected me, Poland accepted me. I have found this syndrome repeated endlessly.

Like many men and women who speculate on these matters, I am impressed by the spell that meaningful but unexplained coincidences play in a long life. For some time I had wanted to discuss the Oliver North case with Frank Shakespeare, and on the morning of the chaotic day on which we were to meet, the *International Herald-Tribune* prints the story which provided the best possible excuse for opening the difficult subject that night. A professor in Poznan unwittingly gives verification of an incident in the life of Jews in Russia. And in the midst of contemplating my own acceptance-rejection in Poland, who should be a fellow celebrant of the pope's private mass that morning in the Vatican but Archbishop Hunthausen, whose case I had followed so intimately because it involved one of the most crucial aspects of my friend Jan Pawel Drugi's occupancy of the papacy.

But mostly I wanted to show how exceedingly full the life of a writer can be as he moves well into his ninth decade.

THE DEEPER
MEANING

*O*bviously this pilgrimage had been a joyous occasion for me, meeting old friends in both Poland and Rome, catching a glimpse of politics in Warsaw and the Vatican, and sensing the important realignments underway in Europe. But the significance of what I was seeing—and in which I was participating—did not strike me until I returned home, for I did not appreciate the wonder of what was happening about me.

Then, in swift and almost bewildering speed, I watched titanic changes occur. The first explosions involved two nations about which I had written and for which I had enormous affection, Hungary and Poland. In what I wrote I had perceived Soviet communism as baleful, and I had doubted that during my lifetime the harsh grip of Russia on the two nations would be relaxed. Indeed, I became involved with the American government through my assignments in waging intellectual warfare against communism and thus, by extension, against the governments of both Hungary and Poland.

With what stunning speed it all changed! Hungary was given the right to hold free elections and install a form of capitalism. It was allowed to tear down the fences that divided it from the free Europe with which it longed to reestablish friendly relations. And most surprising of all, it volunteered to serve as a corridor through which freedom-seeking citizens of Communist East Germany could flee to their brothers in free West Germany. It was a revolution of immense dimension, and it occurred without the firing of a shot. All I had dreamed of as impossible, all I had worked for in the American radios had come to pass, and I felt a surge of joy.

More significant perhaps, because my relations with Poland had been more prolonged and recent—but not more intense than those terrible days of the 1956 Hungarian uprising—were the staggering changes in Poland: the dictator Jaruzelski voluntarily ceding much of his power to a democratic form of government; Lech Walesa triumphant in his long struggle against the Communist establishment; Tadeusz Mazowiecki, a writer who not only defended but also openly espoused Catholic causes installed as prime minister; and a warm breath of freedom replacing the icy chill of communism.

It was a miracle, and I had played a minute part in the transformation, for my novel had inspired the Poles in that country and abroad, and in selecting me to receive the medal of reconciliation from the hands of the then prime minister, the government had sent a signal that it did indeed seek new paths and friendships.

Then, before I had time to catch my breath, other cataclysmic changes took place. The Berlin Wall, that monument to folly, came crashing down. In Romania the unspeakable Ceaucescus, husband and wife, had to be murdered before the nation could be cleansed of their crimes, and even Bulgaria, long the darkest corner of European communism, admitted the light. It was as if a century of history had been compacted into three tumultuous weeks, and men and women throughout the world rejoiced to see the end of an aberrational tyranny. Communism had revealed its bankruptcy; the fight in which I had been engaged had been won.

In the euphoria of victory my thoughts returned to the Vatican and to the stalwart cardinal from Krakow who had fought so long and so valiantly against communism. Joseph Stalin had once asked contemptuously, when told that a former pope had spoken out against Soviet tyrannies, "How many battalions does the pope have?" For nearly half a century that had remained the perceived wisdom: The pope was a spiritual leader, but he did not have to be taken seriously because he had no army to enforce his policies, while communism commanded a vast army prepared to rush into any trouble spot and annihilate dissidents, as had occurred in Hungary in 1956 and Czechoslovakia in 1968. Communism was monolithic and indestructible.

But citizens in the satellite nations remembered what freedom had been. They did not forget their churches and their priests, and when the embers of hope flared into a mighty conflagration, communism collapsed in the ashes. How overjoyed the pope must have been to watch as his religion reestablished itself in his homeland and in the neighboring nations that he knew so well. He led no armed battalions, but he did lead a powerful aggregation of ordinary citizens who longed for freedom and who recovered it.

When we make a pilgrimage we do not travel alone, or naked. We are supported by others of like aspiration and will. We are one of a multitude who bear witness, and if we make no sound as our sandaled feet shuffle along, our voices are nevertheless heard, and we give support to those who cannot march with us or speak in their own defense.

I learned these truths in 1967 when, after a severe illness, I took, upon rising from my bed, the prolonged pilgrimage which travelers in the Middle Ages pursued: Paris to the noble sanctuary at Compostella in northwestern Spain. I was not a Catholic, nor did I believe that the making of that time-honored journey would do me any spiritual good. Put simply, I was writing a book about

Spain and feared it would be incomplete if I missed the importance the Compostella route had exerted on Spanish history and development. But as I traveled the ancient route I began to feel myself one of the pilgrims, and the emotions which had energized them five hundred years ago energized me.

Now my experiences in Poland and Rome entitled me to share the exhilaration of the Poles, Hungarians, Czechoslovakians, Romanians and Bulgarians as they burst forth to freedom. But I also remembered with respect the restrained joy with which the pope greeted the restoration of political and religious freedoms in central and eastern Europe. He did not gloat over the collapse of communism; he gave thanks.

Mine had been a memorable expedition, a peek into the possibilities of the coming century, but I suppose that is why pilgrims always make their journeys: to learn, to participate, to uncover new understandings and to generate new commitments.